Biography Today

Profiles
of People
of Interest
to Young
Readers

Volume 21
Issue 2
April 2012

Cherie D. Abbey
Managing Editor

Omnigraphics

155 West Congress, Suite 200
Detroit, MI 48226

Cherie D. Abbey, *Managing Editor*

Peggy Daniels Becker, Joan Goldsworthy, Kevin Hillstrom, Laurie Hillstrom,
Justin Karr, Leslie Karr, and Diane Telgen, *Sketch Writers*

Allison A. Beckett and Mary Butler, *Research Staff*

* * *

Peter E. Ruffner, *Publisher*
Matthew P. Barbour, *Senior Vice President*

* * *

Elizabeth Collins, *Research and Permissions Coordinator*
Kevin M. Hayes, *Operations Manager*
Cherry Stockdale, *Permissions Assistant*

Shirley Amore, Joseph Harris, Martha Johns,
and Kirk Kauffmann, *Administrative Staff*

Special thanks to Frederick G. Ruffner for creating this series.

Copyright © 2012 EBSCO Publishing, Inc.
ISSN 1058-2347 • ISBN 978-0-7808-1254-3

Library of Congress Cataloging-in-Publication Data

The information in this publication was compiled from sources cited and from
sources considered reliable. While every possible effort has been made to ensure reli-
ability, the publisher will not assume liability for damages caused by inaccuracies in
the data, and makes no warranty, express or implied, on the accuracy of the information contained herein.

This book is printed on acid-free paper meeting the ANSI Z39.48 Standard. The infinity
symbol that appears above indicates that the paper in this book meets that standard.

Printed in the United States

Contents

Preface

Biography Today is a magazine designed and written for the young reader—ages 9 and above—and covers individuals that librarians and teachers tell us that young people want to know about most: entertainers, athletes, writers, illustrators, cartoonists, and political leaders.

The Plan of the Work

The publication was especially created to appeal to young readers in a format they can enjoy reading and readily understand. Each issue contains approximately 10 sketches arranged alphabetically. Each entry provides at least one picture of the individual profiled, and boldfaced rubrics lead the reader to information on birth, youth, early memories, education, first jobs, marriage and family, career highlights, memorable experiences, hobbies, and honors and awards. Each of the entries ends with a list of easily accessible sources designed to lead the student to further reading on the individual and a current address. Retrospective entries are also included, written to provide a perspective on the individual's entire career.

Biographies are prepared by Omnigraphics editors after extensive research, utilizing the most current materials available. Those sources that are generally available to students appear in the list of further reading at the end of the sketch.

Indexes

Cumulative indexes are an important component of *Biography Today*. Each issue of the *Biography Today* General Series includes a Cumulative Names Index, which comprises all individuals profiled in *Biography Today* since the series began in 1992. In addition, we compile three other indexes: the Cumulative General Index, Places of Birth Index, and Birthday Index. See our web site, www.biographytoday.com, for these three indexes, along with the Names Index. All *Biography Today* indexes are cumulative, including all individuals profiled in both the General Series and the Subject Series.

Our Advisors

This series was reviewed by an Advisory Board comprising librarians, children's literature specialists, and reading instructors to ensure that the concept of this publication—to provide a readable and accessible biographical magazine for young readers—was on target. They evaluated the title as it developed, and their suggestions have proved invaluable. Any errors, however, are ours alone. We'd like to list the Advisory Board members and to thank them for their efforts.

Our Advisory Board stressed to us that we should not shy away from controversial or unconventional people in our profiles, and we have tried to follow their advice. The Advisory Board also mentioned that the sketches might be useful in reluctant reader and adult literacy programs, and we would value any comments librarians might have about the suitability of our magazine for those purposes.

Your Comments Are Welcome

Our goal is to be accurate and up to date, to give young readers information they can learn from and enjoy. Now we want to know what you think. Take a look at this issue of *Biography Today*, on approval. Contact me with your comments. We want to provide an excellent source of biographical information for young people. Let us know how you think we're doing.

Cherie Abbey
Managing Editor, *Biography Today*
Omnigraphics, Inc.
155 W. Congress, Suite 200
Detroit, MI 48226
www.omnigraphics.com
editorial@omnigraphics.com

Congratulations!

Congratulations to the following individuals and libraries who are receiving a free copy of *Biography Today*, Vol. 21, No. 2, for suggesting people who appear in this issue.

Carol Arnold, Hoopeston Public Library, Hoopeston, IL

Judi Chelekis, Vassar High School Library, Vassar MI

Sharon Curtis, Phelan Newmarket Elementary School, Newmarket, NH

James P. Hibler, Kalkaska County Library, Grand Rapids, MI

Kimberly Lentz, North Rowan High School, Spencer, NC

Alexis Pedretti, Magnolia Elementary, 6209 Nogales Street, Riverside, CA

Ashley Squires, Charlotte, NC

Owen V., McKenna Elementary School, Massapequa Public Schools, Massapequa, NY

Adele 1988-

British Singer and Songwriter
Grammy-Award Winning Creator of the Hit Albums
19 and *21* and the Songs "Chasing Pavements,"
"Someone Like You," and "Rolling in the Deep"

BIRTH

Adele Laurie Blue Adkins was born on May 5, 1988, in the Tottenham section of North London, England. Her mother, Penny Adkins, was 18 years old when Adele was born. Her mother held various different jobs, including masseuse, artist, and furniture maker. Adele's father, Mark Evans, was a Welsh dockworker who was not involved in raising Adele. She has one half-brother, Cameron, on her father's side.

YOUTH

Adele spent her early childhood years in the Brixton area of South London, near where her mother's family lived. She remembers spending a lot of time with her aunts, uncles, and cousins. "I had, like, 30 cousins living down the road, so I'd go and see them, always arguing and hating to share, then I'd be back home to my tidy room and unbroken toys and no fighting over my Barbie. It was like I had the best of both worlds." When Adele was 11 years old, she and her mother moved to the West Norwood area of South London.

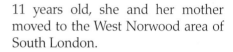

> *Adele grew up as an only child. "I had, like, 30 cousins living down the road, so I'd go and see them, always arguing and hating to share, then I'd be back home to my tidy room and unbroken toys and no fighting over my Barbie. It was like I had the best of both worlds."*

Music was one of Adele's biggest interests while she was growing up. She loved to sing and learned to play guitar and clarinet. "I've always liked being the center of attention," she said. When she was about five years old, she entertained her mother's friends by climbing up on the dinner table and singing "Dreams," a song that was a hit for British pop singer Gabrielle in 1993.

As a young girl, Adele explored a wide variety of music. She liked all sorts of different artists, including Aerosmith, the Backstreet Boys, Mary J. Blige, Billy Bragg, Jeff Buckley, The Cure, Destiny's Child, Aretha Franklin, Marvin Gaye, Korn, the Spice Girls, and Suzanne Vega. Adele never thought about having a career as a singer until she first heard Etta James, an American soul and blues singer. Adele came across an Etta James CD in the bargain bin at a local music store and bought it because she liked the picture on the front. She wanted to show James's hairstyle to her own hairdresser. "Then one day I was cleaning my room and I found it and put it on. When I heard the song 'Fool That I Am,' everything changed for me. I never wanted to be a singer until I heard that."

James became an important influence on Adele. "Etta James is my favorite singer. I've loved her since I was 15," Adele recalled. "Initially it was because I loved the way she looked—the big kinda white-woman weave and

Performing live at the BBC studios, December 2007.

her beautiful, catty eyes! But then, once I actually listened to her, though she didn't really even write any of her own songs, I found that her delivery was just so sincere that she really could convince me she was singing directly to me. Which is something I've never ever found in any other artist. She was the first time a voice made me stop what I was doing and sit down and listen. It took over my mind and body."

For Adele, listening to classic singers like Etta James and Ella Fitzgerald was a revelation. "There was no musical heritage in our family. Chart music was all I ever knew. So when I listened to the Ettas and the Ellas, it sounds so cheesy, but it was like an awakening. I was like, oh, right, some people have proper longevity and are legends. I was so inspired that as a 15-year-old I was listening to music that had been made in the 1940s. The idea that people might look back to my music in 50 years' time was a real spur to doing this."

After that, Adele immersed herself in the music of Etta James and other jazz, soul, and rhythm and blues stars like Ella Fitzgerald, Roberta Flack, Jill Scott, and Peggy Lee. She was fascinated by their talent for vocal improvisation, or scat singing. Scat singing is the art of singing with nonsense syllables, or sounds with no words at all. This gives the singer the ability to improvise a vocal solo performance. Adele wanted to learn the technique, and she studied the way these singers used improvisation to add to their recordings.

EDUCATION

Adele attended public schools in London, England. In secondary school, she wanted to join the school choir but was told by the music director that she was not good enough. A friend of her mother's suggested that Adele apply to attend The BRIT School for Performing Arts in London. This prestigious school for the arts was attended by many famous British musicians, including Amy Winehouse and Leona Lewis.

"When I was 14, all my friends were getting pregnant. I panicked, and I was like, 'I don't want this to happen to me.' I applied to school more as a way out than anything," Adele recalled. "As soon as I got a microphone in my hand, when I was about 14, I realized I wanted to do this. Most people don't like the way their voice sounds when it's recorded. I was just so excited by the whole thing that I wasn't bothered by what it sounded like."

Adele auditioned for and was accepted to The BRIT School. She has suggested that enrolling in courses there changed her life and set her on the right path to build a successful career as a singer and songwriter. "I think I do owe it completely to The BRIT School for making me who I am today, as cheesy and embarrassing as it may sound. Because, while my mum is the most supportive mum on Earth, she wouldn't have known how to channel me. With her I'd probably have gone down the classical music route, or maybe Disney, or musical theater ... but at The BRIT School I found my direction, because the music course was really wicked. It had free rehearsal rooms with free equipment, where I was listening to music all day for years. It's not your typical stage-school full of kids that are pushed into it by their parents. It's a school full of kids that will dance at a freezing cold town hall barefoot for eight hours solid. And, whereas before I was going to a school with bums and kids that were rude and wanted to grow up and mug people, it was really inspiring to wake up every day to go to school with kids that actually wanted to be productive at something and wanted to be somebody." Adele graduated from The BRIT School in 2006.

CAREER HIGHLIGHTS

A few months after graduation, Adele posted some of her original songs on the web and began to attract attention. Soon she was performing small gigs around London. She first appeared on stage in 2006 as the opening act for her friend Jack Peñate, a British singer and songwriter. There were about 100 people in the audience. "I went on first and I was on my own, and the whole room was packed. It was hot. It was disgusting," Adele remembered. She started to sing, and "the whole room was silent, and I saw these random girls just, like, crying. That was the time I was like, 'Oh my

God, this is amazing, can't live without it.' There's nothing more freeing than playing live, nothing."

Adele signed her first recording contract in 2006. A year later she released her debut singles, "Hometown Glory" and "Chasing Pavements." Adele wrote "Hometown Glory," one of the first songs she ever wrote, an ode to the city of London. She was inspired to write "Chasing Pavements" after a horrible breakup with her boyfriend. They got into an argument in a bar and Adele ran out. "I was running down these gigantic, wide sidewalks that stretch on for miles, thinking to myself, 'Where are you going? What are you doing? You're just chasing pavements … that you're never going to catch.' Then, I went straight home and wrote the song."

A Successful Debut Album: *19*

In 2008, Adele released *19,* her first full-length album. The album's title refers to her age at the time. Though she had written a few songs when she was younger, Adele did not have the confidence to create a whole album until after she signed her recording contract. "I didn't realize this was something I could do until I got my record deal," she explained. "When I was signed at 18, I only had three songs to my name. But yet, literally within a month of turning 19, a load more just suddenly came out of me."

"My debut album is about being between 18 and 19, about love," Adele said. "It's quite a sad album, being cheated on and not getting what you want." The songs on *19* are about love, loss, and the thoughts and feelings that come after a relationship ends. "Apart from 'Hometown Glory', 'Daydreamer', and 'My Same'—which were all written earlier, when I was between 16 and 18—the whole album is all about one boy. So I was very sad when I wrote it. And I think that genuinely does come through in the music."

19 was an instant success in the United Kingdom. The album debuted in the No. 1 position on the British music charts, and Adele sold out her first

> *"At The BRIT School I found my direction, because the music course was really wicked. It had free rehearsal rooms with free equipment, where I was listening to music all day for years…. It was really inspiring to wake up every day to go to school with kids that actually wanted to be productive at something and wanted to be somebody."*

Appearing on "Saturday Night Live," her first big introduction
to the U.S. audience, October 2008.

United Kingdom tour as a headlining act. In recognition of her success, she received the first ever Critics' Choice Brit Award in 2008. *19* was released in the United States six months later, and Adele began her first U.S. tour.

American music fans were slower to embrace Adele, until she was the musical guest on an episode of the popular television show "Saturday Night Live" in October 2008, shortly before the 2008 presidential election. Adele had the good fortune of appearing on the same episode of the show as Sarah Palin, who was at that time the Republican candidate for vice president. A controversial candidate, Palin had been the subject of several sketch parodies by Tina Fey on "Saturday Night Live." So when Palin herself appeared on the show, millions of extra viewers tuned in to see the politician—and also heard the new singer Adele. After the show aired, her album quickly rose to No. 10 on the *Billboard* 200 music chart. *19* soon became a Top Internet Album and a Top Digital Album as well.

As *19* grew in popularity, Adele attracted fans across musical genres. Her soulful delivery of bluesy songs captivated listeners looking for something different. Adele attributed the success of *19* to the widespread accessibility and appeal of soul music. "What I particularly like about soul and blues is its honesty, sincerity, and depth. While with pop, though you do have the entertainment factor, when you scratch away the surface there's very little underneath. Whereas with soul you can constantly trawl through it and find great new things. To me the most important thing, in terms of longevity, is to be real in your music. And soul and blues are filled with real, proper emotions. Like every time I hear Lauryn Hill's voice, she makes me cry."

19 ultimately earned four Grammy Award nominations in 2009: Best New Artist, and Best Female Vocal Pop Performance, Record of the Year, and Song of the Year, all for "Chasing Pavements." Adele was shocked to find that she won the Grammy Awards for Best New Artist and Best Female Vocal Pop Performance. Sitting in the audience during the long awards program, Adele was so convinced that she would not win that by the time her name was called, she had already taken off her shoes and her belt.

The runaway success of *19* caught Adele by surprise. "It didn't even occur to me that a million-plus people would hear my record, and that people were gonna love it and criticize it. And it kind of frightens me sometimes 'cause I think my record's really honest—there's things in it that I'd never admitted to myself, that I would never just say in conversation. But then the other side of it is that I always get people coming up to me after shows and telling me that it helped them through their relationship at the time, which is an amazing feeling," she said. "It's really cheesy, but I feel like I'm living the dream. Even if nothing at all happened for me after 2008, I can say I've done it once and it's been amazing."

A Record-Breaking Follow-Up: *21*

In 2011, Adele released *21*, her second album. The album's title again reflected her age at the time. *21* quickly became the biggest selling album of the year, with millions of copies sold in the first few months alone. By February 2012, *21* had spent a total of 21 weeks at the top of American music charts. Ironically, the album *21* sold more than 730,000 copies in week 21 on the charts, the most copies sold in a single week. *Daily Variety* music reviewer A.J. Marechal acknowledged Adele's star power by writing, "Whether in the recording studio or on stage, Adele belts with the kind of emotional depth seldom seen in today's era of mega-production tours. The lyrical honesty of such heartbreak-inspired songs as 'Someone Like You' paired with a powerful voice known to hush celeb-filled rooms has translated into big numbers."

The single "Rolling in the Deep" became a huge crossover hit on Adult Contemporary, R&B/Hip Hop, and Alternative radio stations. The song occupied the No. 1 position on the *Billboard* Hot 100 music chart for eight weeks. With record-breaking digital sales, "Rolling in the Deep" propelled

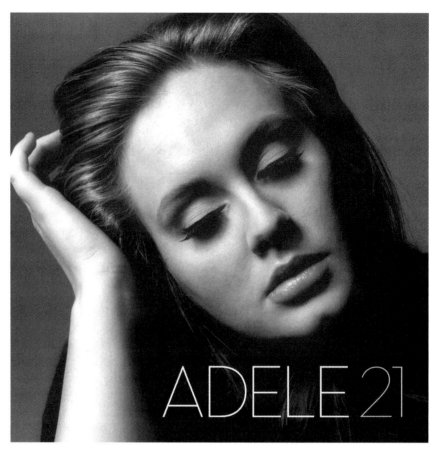

21 was Adele's big breakthrough album.

21 to Top Digital Album status. Music lovers around the world bought more than 10 million copies of *21*. More than 15,000 cover versions and remixes of "Rolling in the Deep" were uploaded to YouTube. The official music video for "Rolling in the Deep" was viewed more than 121 million times on YouTube. These numbers were not only record-breaking, but unprecedented. National Public Radio commentator Sami Yenigun observed, "Simply put, 'Rolling in the Deep' is a heart-stopping, chart-topping, YouTube popping, cover-propping, booty-dropping jam. The song of the summer."

Music critics were generous in their praise. *San Francisco Chronicle* reviewer David Wagner praised Adele's talent by writing, "This is a voice with such emotional resonance that it could sing the Oscar Mayer bologna jingle and still reduce hardened criminals to tears." *Minneapolis Star-Tribune* reviewer Jon Bream noted that "Adele favors a less-is-more style.... She's all about making the listener feel the pain—all her songs are sad except for one or two—without her screaming. It's controlled anger, delivered with deeply soulful aches, an occasional crack and a hint of weariness. She knows how to hold her notes a beat longer to underscore the fervor of her emotion."

In recognition of her phenomenal success with *21*, Adele was nominated for four American Music Awards in 2011, including Artist of the Year. She won the awards for Favorite Pop/Rock Female Artist, Favorite Adult Contemporary Artist, and Favorite Pop/Rock Album, for *21*. In 2011, Adele received three Teen Choice Awards, including Choice Music Female Artist, Choice Breakout Artist, and Choice Break Up Song, for "Rolling in the Deep." "Rolling in the Deep"was named MTV's Song of the Year for 2011, and was nominated for seven MTV Video Music Awards, winning three. Adele was also nominated for four 2012 People's Choice Awards, including two for "Rolling in the Deep"and one for the album *21*.

"What I particularly like about soul and blues is its honesty, sincerity, and depth. While with pop, though you do have the entertainment factor, when you scratch away the surface there's very little underneath.... To me the most important thing, in terms of longevity, is to be real in your music. And soul and blues are filled with real, proper emotions."

A Health Crisis

During her 2011 tour, Adele began to suffer from a mysterious vocal ailment. Her voice had been weakened when she came down with the flu in late 2010, and in early 2011 she found that she suddenly could not sing at all. She was diagnosed with severe laryngitis and ordered to rest her voice completely for 10 days. (Laryngitis is swelling of the voice box, or larynx, that results in extreme hoarseness or loss of voice.) Her voice improved with rest and Adele was able to speak and sing again, as long as she followed a strict program of vocal rest, vocal warm up exercises, and specific food and drinks.

But just a few months later, in the middle of a conversation, Adele's voice simply "switched off like a light." Unable to speak or sing, she was diagnosed with a hemorrhage on her vocal cords. (A hemorrhage refers to bleeding caused by a broken blood vessel.) Her doctors told her that if she continued trying to sing, she might do permanent damage and lose her

Adele is known for her powerful singing style in live performances.

voice forever. This terrible news came in the middle of her U.S. tour. Adele reluctantly canceled performances and took a month off to rest. Writing on her blog, she explained, "Singing is literally my life, it's my hobby, my love, my freedom, and now my job. I have absolutely no choice but to recuperate properly and fully, or I risk damaging my voice forever."

After that period of rest, Adele was able to continue on with her tour performances and other commitments. In late 2011, however, she experienced another hemorrhage and was forced to cancel the rest of her tour in the U.S. and the United Kingdom. Adele underwent surgery on her vocal cords in November 2011. Within a month after the surgery, she resumed vocal training and was able to begin singing again, with strict limitations. "The surgery couldn't have gone better. But because I was singing with damaged vocal cords for three or four months and because of the surgery and because of the silence after the surgery I now have to build myself back up vocally. It's gonna be a lot easier for me to sing now."

By February 2012, Adele's recovery was complete and she was able to return to the stage. Her first public performance after surgery was during the 2012 Grammy Awards show, where she gave a powerful performance of "Rolling in the Deep" that brought the Grammy audience—filled with top performers—to its feet. She also collected six Grammy Awards: she won the awards for Record of the Year, Song of the Year, and Best Short Form Music Video for "Rolling in the Deep," Album of the Year and Best Pop Vocal Album for *21*, and Best Pop Solo Performance for "Someone Like You." She went on to win two Brit Awards, for British Female Solo Artist and British Album of the Year, for *21*.

Adele's future plans include writing new songs and recording a new album. She plans to take as much time as she needs to make the best record she can. "I imagine I'll be 25 or 26 by the time my next record comes out, as I haven't even thought about my third record yet. I'll disappear and come back with a record when it's good enough. There will be no new music until it's good enough and until I'm ready."

HOME AND FAMILY

Adele lives in London, England, with her mother and her dog, a dachshund named Louis Armstrong.

SELECTED RECORDINGS

19, 2008
21, 2011

HONORS AND AWARDS

Brit Awards (British Phonographic Institute): 2008, Critics' Choice; 2012 (two awards), British Female Solo Artist and British Album of the Year, for *21*

Grammy Awards: 2009 (two awards), Best New Artist Award and Best Female Vocal Pop Performance, for "Chasing Pavements"; 2012 (six awards), Record of the Year, Song of the Year, and Best Short Form Music Video, for "Rolling in the Deep," Album of the Year and Best Pop Vocal Album, for *21*, Best Pop Solo Performance, for "Someone Like You"

American Music Awards: 2011 (three awards), Favorite Adult Contemporary Artist, Favorite Pop/Rock Female Artist, and Favorite Pop/Rock Album, for *21*

MTV Song of the Year: 2011, for "Rolling in the Deep"

MTV Video Music Awards: 2011 (three awards), Best Art Direction in a Video, Best Cinematography in a Video, and Best Editing in a Video, all for "Rolling in the Deep"

Teen Choice Awards: 2011 (three awards), Choice Music Female Artist, Choice Breakout Artist, and Choice Break Up Song, for "Rolling in the Deep"

FURTHER READING

Periodicals

Billboard, Dec. 17, 2011
Current Biography Yearbook, 2009
Entertainment Weekly, Apr. 15, 2011, p.56; July 1, 2011, p.16
Glamour, Dec. 2008, p.270
Marie Claire, Feb. 2011, p.113
People, May 16, 2011, p. 56
Rolling Stone, Apr. 28, 2011, p.52; Sep. 15, 2011, p.13
USA Today, Feb. 18, 2011
Vogue, Apr. 2009, p.198

Online Articles

www.bbc.co.uk
    (BBC News, "How Has Adele Become So Successful?"Mar. 28, 2011)
www.billboard.biz
    (Billboard, "21 and Up: Adele's Billboard Cover Story,"Dec. 8, 2011)
www.bluesandsoul.com
    (Blues and Soul, "Adele: Up Close and Personal,"no date)
www.mtv.com/music/artists
    (MTV, "Adele,"no date)
www.rollingstone.com
    (Rolling Stone, "Adele Opens Up about Her Inspirations, Looks, and
    Stage Fright in New *Rolling Stone* Cover Story, Apr. 13, 2011)
www.vh1.com/artists/az/adele/artist.jhtml
    (VH1, "Adele,"no date)

ADDRESS

Adele
Columbia Records
550 Madison Ave., 24th Floor
New York, NY 10022

WEB SITE

www.adele.tv

Chris Daughtry 1979-
American Rock Musician
Lead Singer of Daughtry
Fourth-Place "American Idol" Finalist

Editor's Note: Daughtry is the leader of the rock group of the same name, so using that name can be confusing. Throughout this article, the name "Chris" is used to refer to the individual, and the name "Daughtry" is used to refer to the group as a whole.

BIRTH

Christopher Adam Daughtry was born on December 26, 1979, in Roanoke Rapids, North Carolina, just south of the Virginia border. His parents, Pete and Sandra Daughtry, raised Chris and his older brother, Kenneth, in Lasker, North Carolina.

YOUTH

Chris was raised in the backwoods of North Carolina. From the time he was a toddler, he grew up picking potatoes and corn on the family farm, where his family kept chickens, goats, ducks, and hunting dogs. As a child, he was interested in martial arts and dreamed of starring in action movies like Jean-Claude Van Damme. He was also a fan of professional wrestling, which he would watch on television with his dad. In addition, he was an avid reader of comic books and showed some artistic talent. He spent his spare time drawing in hopes of becoming a comic book artist.

When Chris was 14, the Daughtry family moved to Lake Monticello, Virginia. As a teenager, he enjoyed a range of music. He started listening to 1990s grunge and rock bands like Pearl Jam, Alice in Chains, Soundgarden, Stone Temple Pilots, and Live. He also admired rap music by Public Enemy, N.W.A., and the Beastie Boys and enjoyed heavy metal music by Guns n' Roses and Skid Row. At age 16 he learned to play the guitar and started to take his singing voice seriously, performing in various rock bands during his high school years.

EDUCATION

Chris attended Fluvanna County High School in Palmyra, Virginia, graduating in 1998. He found his calling as a performer in school productions of the musicals *The Wiz* and *Peter Pan*. His first live solo performance was at his grandfather's bar, where he sang "Achy Breaky Heart" for a crowd of locals. During his junior year, his math teacher offered extra credit to any student who wrote something math-related—such as a poem—and shared it with the class. Chris and his friend Rob Nesbit wrote and performed a math song; it was such a hit that they were asked to perform it for other math classes. Nesbit told the *Fluvanna Review* that he taught Chris "some chords and how to put songs together" on the guitar. Soon after, Chris formed the band Cadence, for which he sang lead vocals and played rhythm guitar. The band recorded a very rare album entitled *All Eyes on You* in 1999 and performed live on a local college radio station.

FIRST JOBS

Chris held several jobs as a teenager. He started working with his father in a sawmill at age 14 and later worked at McDonald's, Lowe's Home Improvement, and an appliance rental center. After high school, he moved to

McLeansville, North Carolina, and got a job behind the service desk at a Honda dealership in Greensboro. "I got on my boss's nerves a lot. I'd always be in my own head, trying to write a song,"he remembered. At that time, he was the front man for his band, Absent Element, which recorded an album, *Uprooted,* in 2005. The CD includes the tracks "Conviction"and "Breakdown," which the singer would later combine and re-record as "Breakdown" on his self-titled debut album.

Absent Element performed regularly at several local bars. Despite these weekend gigs, Chris's day job and family commitments prevented him from taking the conventional route to a career in the music business. "I couldn't just hop in a van and play places until you get noticed,"he explained. "I didn't have that luxury. It was just,'I'm gonna play here, and hopefully somebody that means something will come along and snag me up.'But that never happened, so it was,'All right, I gotta do it on TV instead.'" In 2005 he auditioned for "Rock Star: INXS"—a reality-show competition to discover a new lead singer for the Australian rock band INXS—but did not advance to the televised round.

As a struggling musician, Chris couldn't afford to quit his day job. "I couldn't just hop in a van and play places until you get noticed," he explained. "I didn't have that luxury. It was just, 'I'm gonna play here, and hopefully somebody that means something will come along and snag me up.'"

CAREER HIGHLIGHTS

"American Idol"

In winter 2006 Chris and approximately 9,000 other contestants auditioned for the fifth season of the Fox television talent show "American Idol" in Denver, Colorado. "I thought to myself,'How am I gonna stand out?'" he recalled. He passed the preliminary round in front of the show's producers and then was invited to sing for a minute or so in front of the judges, Paula Abdul, Simon Cowell, and Randy Jackson. His goal at that stage was to wow the judges and earn a ticket to Hollywood to appear on the show. Chris chose to sing "The Letter," written by country musician Wayne Carson Thompson. The song has been performed by several artists, including British rock singer Joe Cocker, upon whose rendition Chris based his performance. Jackson immediately liked him, complimenting his voice and his stylistic choices. Cowell, however, criticized him for rushing

Chris with the cast of "American Idol," season five.

the song and showing a lack of charisma. "I'm not sure I'm looking at a standalone star," he observed, voting against Chris. Abdul agreed with Jackson: "I heard talent, and I saw nerves. But I like you." With the support of Abdul and Jackson, Chris advanced to the televised competition. He left the audition room with a golden ticket to Hollywood tucked under his cowboy hat.

Season Five of "American Idol" began in February 2006, and Chris quickly became a fan favorite. He performed Bon Jovi's "Dead or Alive" for his first national TV appearance and songs by the rock bands Fuel and Seether the following two weeks. "He was different than the typical 'Idol' style," said executive producer Ken Warwick in *Entertainment Weekly.* "Chris had attitude and credibility. He didn't sell himself out during the show." Later in the competition, he performed a hard rock version of Johnny Cash's "Walk the Line" as well as hits by Stevie Wonder, Louis Armstrong, Bryan Adams, and Styx. As a reviewer said in *Entertainment Weekly,* "The bald boy can tackle the perilous theme nights—from Stevie Wonder to country—and still give performances that are undeniably his…. Chris gives us what we are hungry for." The judges and audience embraced him, and the tabloid press predicted he would win the competition based on both talent and his physical resemblance to action film star Vin Diesel. As Chuck Arnold and Carrie Borzillo-Vrenna stated in *People,* "His cred as a bona-fide rocker—plus that whole Vin Diesel thing—many give him the best shot at true idoldom."

After competing for 13 weeks, Chris was one of four singers still standing in the contest that *Entertainment Weekly* deemed "the biggest 'Idol' (season) ever." Indeed, Season Five lacked a clear frontrunner, featuring such gifted performers as Elliott Yamin, Katharine McPhee, Kellie Pickler, and Taylor Hicks. During the semi-finals on May 9, 2006, Chris sang the Elvis Presley hits "Suspicious Minds" and "A Little Less Conversation," drawing rave reviews from the judges. "See ya in the finals," Abdul hinted after his stirring performances. The next night, however, "American Idol" host Ryan Seacrest delivered the news that shocked the contestants, judges, and viewers. "A lot of people predicted, Chris, that you could be the next 'American Idol,'" Seacrest announced. "Chris, you are going home tonight. This journey ends."

"He was different than the typical 'Idol' style," said executive producer Ken Warwick. "Chris had attitude and credibility. He didn't sell himself out during the show."

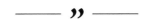

Chris finished the "American Idol" competition in fourth place. After the surprising revelation that viewers had voted him off the show, several audience members booed the decision. His fans were in tears, as was one of the judges. "Randy was pretty much saying, 'Don't worry about it, you're going to be fine.' Paula was crying too much to say anything," Chris recalled. "And Simon was shocked. He said he didn't see this coming and wished me the best of luck and totally believes in me." Although Chris has admitted that it was a gut-wrenching, unexpected moment, he did not dwell on his loss for long. "It didn't feel good but I try to look at the positive and see the bigger picture and say, 'You know what? Maybe this is the right thing. Maybe this is just a big opportunity for many doors to open,'" he said.

Chris did not have to wait long for the next opportunity to present itself. Hours after he was eliminated from "American Idol," he got a surprising proposal: members of the band Fuel made a pitch to him on the TV show "Extra" and offered him a job as their lead singer. During the second week of "American Idol," Chris had sung a rendition of the Fuel song "Hemorrhage (In My Hands)" that caught the band's attention and renewed the public's interest in the group. Although Chris was flattered by the offer and seriously considered it, he ultimately decided to turn it down in favor of

Performing live on "American Idol," March 2006.

launching a solo career. "Deep down, I knew it wasn't for me," he admitted. "I wasn't comfortable being the guy who replaced the other guy or being limited to their success. I wanted to create my own. If I failed, I could blame myself." The media has often asked him whether he regrets any of the choices he made on "American Idol," to which he has responded,

"Nothing on the show hurt my confidence.... That's one reason I did so well. I didn't let them sway me or change me in any way. I think that's the key to anything in life: You have to know who you are."

Daughtry

Chris was soon glad he trusted his instincts, when he was asked to perform the original song "Home" for legendary record producer Clive Davis in his office at 19 Recordings/RCA Records. "He was the first Idol that I'd ever met who had material that he had written," Davis said in *Entertainment Weekly.* "That was compelling." In July 2006 Chris signed a contract with Davis's record label and began working on material for his debut album in collaboration with such A-list songwriters as Rob Thomas of Matchbox Twenty, Mitch Allan of SR-71, and Carl Bell of Fuel. Meanwhile, his rendition of Bon Jovi's hit "Wanted Dead or Alive" was released as a single, debuting at No. 43 on *Billboard*'s Hot 100 list and No. 16 on its Hot Digital Tracks list.

The self-titled debut *Daughtry* was released in November 2006, just six months after he left "American Idol." Featuring 12 tracks, all but two of which Chris had a hand in writing, *Daughtry* became the fastest-selling rock debut album in Nielsen SoundScan history. *Billboard* magazine declared it the top-selling album of 2007 with almost 2.3 million copies sold. Moreover, the album reached No. 1 on the *Billboard* Top 200 chart and spawned three No. 1 singles: "It's Not Over," "Home," and "Feels Like Tonight." By 2008 *Daughtry* had sold more than four million copies.

Despite impressive sales figures, critical reviews of Daughtry were mixed. Although most commentators praised Chris's voice and songwriting abilities, some characterized the album as monotonous and generic. For example, critic Henry Goldblatt deemed the song "It's Not Over" "ridiculously catchy" in *Entertainment Weekly,* describing Chris's voice as "a confident sultry growl that's not pitch-perfect, but pretty close." Later in the review, however, he lamented the album's lack of variety. Likewise, commentator Stephen Thomas Erlewine in *All Music Guide* extolled Chris's vocal range and the sensitivity in his singing, describing his songs as "sturdier than most post-grunge, with big, anthemic hooks on the choruses." Chris received some recognition at the 2007 American Music Awards where he received three awards, for favorite contemporary artist, favorite breakthrough new artist, and favorite pop/rock album. "We were certainly new to the industry, but getting recognized for your hard work is a pretty big deal," he acknowledged. The following month he was nominated for four Grammy awards.

Chris had recorded his debut album using studio musicians. But as he prepared to go out on tour to promote the album, he held auditions for permanent band members. The group, which goes by the name Daughtry, features Josh Steely and Brian Craddock on guitar, Josh Paul on bass, and Robin Diaz on drums (original guitarist Jeremy Brady and drummer Joey Barnes are no longer in the band). "We're just normal guys who are doing what we've always wanted to do and what we love to do," Chris affirmed. Asked why he named the band Daughtry, he joked, "Because I'm conceited. Just kidding. It was more about name recognition than anything else." The band has been performing live all over the world since 2007, embarking on a sold-out tour with Bon Jovi in 2008. Opening for Bon Jovi was a turning point for Chris. "At the end of the tour Jon did this speech in Atlanta ... and at the end of it he says,'This man will never open for another band again.'To get that respect from someone who has obviously stayed relevant for that amount of time? It felt really good."

Leave This Town

While on the road, Chris and the band began working on songs for the next Daughtry record. The resulting album, *Leave This Town,* was released in July 2009. In addition to powerful anthems, quiet ballads, and emotional mid-tempo tracks, the album includes a country-influenced tune, "Tennessee Line," which features harmonies by country music sensation Vince Gill. The album's title comes from a line in the song "September," a bittersweet ballad inspired by Chris's childhood experiences growing up with his brother in small-town North Carolina. The anthem "No Surprise" became the group's fourth No. 1 single.

Chris worked with band members Steely and Craddock to write many of the tunes on *Leave This Town,* and he also collaborated with Mitch Allan from SR-71 and Chad Kroeger from Nickelback. "We went in together as a band and wrote the record together, arranged the songs together in rehearsals, and recorded them all together," Chris remarked. "It was very much a collaborative effort, as opposed to ... having to rush to record [the first album] with studio musicians." His vision guided each recording and he co-wrote all 12 of the songs on the album. Still, Chris emphasized that "[Leave This Town] will definitely show people that it is a band and not a one-man show.... It's a rock band, it's definitely not all me up there."

Leave This Town opened at the top of the *Billboard* 200 chart upon its release in July 2009, selling 269,000 copies in its first week. As a result, Chris became the first "American Idol" contestant to produce two consecutive No. 1 albums. Again, critical reviews were mixed. "*Leave This Town* might not make an impression on those not already inclined to love it," wrote

Daughtry's 2009 album Leave This Town.

Ann Powers in the *Los Angeles Times,* "but Daughtry is still a major architect in mainstream rock, and his music is part of an important shift in the genre.... Dismiss him at your peril."Reviewers also acknowledged that he was attuned to his audience. "[Chris Daughtry] is a man of straightforward meat-and-potatoes rock principle, and so far it's served him very well," Leah Greenblatt argued in *Entertainment Weekly.* "One may search *Town* in vain for a flash of something raw and off-the-script, a moment that does not feel both scrupulously test-marketed and impeccably (over)produced, but Daughtry's relentless competence as a mainstream-rock artist likely serves him far better than any radical departure ever could."

In 2009 the band made a number of high-profile appearances, including performances at the American Music Awards, the Country Music Awards, Dick Clark's New Year's Rockin' Eve with Ryan Seacrest, and the Dallas

Chris with the band Daughtry.

Cowboys game on Thanksgiving Day. In fall 2009 they launched a headlining arena tour across the United States.

Break the Spell

The third album, *Break the Spell,* came out in November 2011. "We came up with some pretty interesting tunes that sound nothing like anything we've done before," Chris pointed out. "Even though some of them didn't make the album, the process stretched us and took us to new places. It was an absolutely inspirational experience." In spite of the lukewarm reception by critics, the album debuted at No. 8 on the *Billboard* 200 with sales of 129,000 in its first week.

Again, reviews were mixed. Brian Mansfield of *USA Today* argued that "*Break the Spell*" doesn't break the Daughtry mold, but it does find the group stretching out a bit. The earnest, angst-ridden rockers are still there, in the title track and early single 'Crawling Back to You,' but songs like 'Rescue Me' and 'Gone Too Soon' broaden the band's sound." Writing in *Billboard*, music critic Gary Graff commented that "[*Break the Spell*] isn't quite all things for all people. But it comes pretty close. The quintet brings its best Bon Jovi-style power drive on rockers like 'Renegade,' 'Outta My Head,' and 'Louder Than Ever.'... The real wrinkle on *Break the Spell*, however, is a more substantive and deliberate embrace of country crossover.... It all sounds sturdy and fits comfortably down the middle, more dependable than daring." Other commentators were less generous. Jonathan Keefe argued in *Slant Magazine* that "[*Break the Spell*] reaffirms that the band is defined by competence rather than ambition or creativity, by rote expressions of overwrought emotions rather than insight or depth." Despite such comments, Daughtry has remained a big hit with fans and has sold more than seven million albums.

Chris is regarded as a devoted family man. Now that he has a successful career in music, his biggest challenge is balancing fame and family. "I don't want to look back and think that I missed opportunities to make memories with my kids," he stated.

MARRIAGE AND FAMILY

Chris has been married to Deanna Robertson since he was 20 years old. The couple met at a party and wed six months later, on November 11, 2000. "We had an instant connection," he recalled. At the time of their marriage, Deanna, a massage therapist, had two children from previous relationships: Hannah, born in 1996; and Griffin, born in 1998. In 2010, Chris and Deanna welcomed fraternal twins, daughter Adalynn Rose and son Noah James. As a father of teens and toddlers, Chris says, "It's pretty crazy having to take [Hannah and Griffin] to this lesson and see this friend, and this and that. And then you have the one-year-olds, who are completely needy! They can't do anything for themselves—it's ridiculous! They're so awesome, though." The family lives in Oak Ridge, North Carolina, with three dogs, a guinea pig, and chickens as pets.

Chris is regarded as a devoted family man, and many consider this to be one of his most admirable qualities. "It wasn't like, 'This is cool that I'm a rock guy taking on two kids,'" he explained. "It just felt like that was what I was supposed to do." Now that Chris has a successful career in music, his biggest challenge is balancing fame and family. "I don't want to look back and think that I missed opportunities to make memories with my kids," he stated. Although he has an impressive list of accomplishments, he has cited "teaching my son to ride a bike" as one of his proudest moments. He has acknowledged that being away from home has been difficult.

HOBBIES AND OTHER INTERESTS

Chris values quality time spent with his family above all else. He enjoys such family activities as taking his kids to the movies and helping them make Halloween costumes; he is even known to dress up like Batman from time to time. He still enjoys drawing, painting, and comic books, especially the Spider-Man and Batman franchises. He is very active on Twitter, where he converses with friends, family, and fans.

Since becoming a celebrity, Chris has demonstrated a commitment to giving back to the community through charitable work. He has been involved in a number of fundraisers, including the ONE Campaign to fight poverty and AIDS in Africa. He has given special concerts for a variety of groups, including the ONE Campaign, children's hospitals, and servicemen and women on military bases all over the world. Despite this demanding schedule, Chris has insisted that he is "just an easygoing, lighthearted guy." Of his life as a rock star, he has said: "It's go, go, go, but I wanted to do this my whole life, so I'm enjoying every minute of it."

RECORDINGS

Daughtry, 2006
Leave This Town, 2009
Break the Spell, 2011

HONORS AND AWARDS

American Music Awards: 2007, Favorite Adult Contemporary Artist, Favorite Breakthrough New Artist, Favorite Pop/Rock Album, for *Daughtry*; 2008, Favorite Pop/Rock Band/Duo/Group
People's Choice Awards: 2008, Favorite Rock Song, for "Home"

FURTHER READING

Books

Marcovitz, Hal. *American Idol Superstars: Chris Daughtry,* 2010

Periodicals

Billboard, Dec. 22, 2007, p.54; June 20, 2009, p.21
Entertainment Weekly, Feb. 23, 2007, p.72
Newsweek, July 20, 2009, p.66
Rolling Stone, Apr. 5, 2007, p.30
Time, Jan. 21, 2008, p.19
Today's Woman, Dec. 2009, p.66
USA Today, Mar. 21, 2007, p.D1

Online Articles

www.allmusic.com
    (Allmusic, "Artist: Daughtry,"undated)
www.billboard.com
    (Billboard, "The *Billboard* Q&A: Chris Daughtry,"Dec. 22, 2007)
www.ew.com
    (Entertainment Weekly, "The Anti-Idol,"Feb. 23, 2007)
www.gibson.com
    (Gibson, "It's Daughtry's World; We Just Shop in It,"Sep. 17, 2007; "The
    Gibson Classic Interview: Chris Daughtry,"Feb. 19, 2011)
www.knowtheartist.com
    (KnowTheArtist, "Daughtry to *Leave This Town,"*Aug. 14, 2009)
www.time.com
    (Time, "Q & A: Talking with Chris Daughtry,"Jan. 21, 2008)

ADDRESS

Chris Daughtry
RCA Records
550 Madison Ave.
New York, NY 10022

WEB SITES

www.daughtryofficial.com
www.rcarecords.com/artists/daughtry
www.americanidol.com/archive/contestants/season5/chris_daughtry

Dale Earnhardt Jr. 1974-

American Professional Race Car Driver
Nine-Time Winner of NASCAR's Most Popular
Driver Award

BIRTH

Ralph Dale Earnhardt Jr. (known to auto racing fans as Dale Jr.
or just Junior) was born on October 10, 1974, in Kannapolis,
North Carolina. His parents were Ralph Dale Earnhardt Sr.
(known as Dale), a professional race car driver, and his second
wife, Brenda Gee Earnhardt. Dale Earnhardt Sr. was married
three times and had four children. Dale Jr. has a sister, Kelley,
who is two years older. He also has an older half-brother,

Kerry, from his father's first marriage, and a younger half-sister, Taylor, from his father's third marriage.

YOUTH

Auto racing was a huge part of Dale Jr.'s life from an early age. The town where he was born, about 30 miles outside of Charlotte, was nicknamed "Car Town" because all of the streets were named after car models or engine parts. In addition, many of the people who lived and worked in the area were involved with the National Association for Stock Car Auto Racing (NASCAR).

Stock car racing got its start in the American South after World War II ended in 1945. Young men bought regular street cars and modified the engines to make them go faster. Then they held informal races on country roads and oval dirt tracks across the region. This type of racing was called "stock" car racing because the cars were souped-up versions of the ones sold in automobile dealerships, rather than specially built racing machines. In the late 1940s, a group of racers formed NASCAR to organize races and award prizes to the winners. NASCAR eventually grew into the largest sanctioning body for the sport of stock car racing, with drivers in various divisions competing in 1,500 races at 100 different tracks each year. NASCAR's highest division is the Sprint Cup (formerly known as the Winston Cup and the Nextel Cup), followed by the Nationwide Series (formerly known as the Busch Series).

> **"**
>
> *"[Dad] never really did anything with me. He never told me things. We were raised by six or seven nannies. I always thought he felt I wasn't much like him,"* Dale Jr. recalled. *"He was intimidating, like they say. He was like that as a father when he was at home. You wanted to please him all the time, make him happy, and you wanted to somehow get a response from him."*
>
> **"**

Dale Jr. was born into a NASCAR family. His paternal grandfather, Ralph Earnhardt, was a legendary driver who won more than 500 races in the early days of NASCAR. His maternal grandfather, Robert Gee, was a well-known car builder and mechanic for NASCAR race teams. His father, Dale Sr., was an up-and-coming young driver at the time of Dale Jr.'s birth. He eventually became one of the most popular and successful drivers in NASCAR history, winning 76 Winston Cup races and seven champi-

Dale Sr. and family celebrating a win in 1985. From left: Kelley, Dale Jr.'s sister; Dale Sr.; Teresa, Dale Jr.'s stepmother; and Dale Jr.

onships during his 25-year career. Several uncles, cousins, and other members of the extended family worked in the racing industry as well.

Feeling Distant from His Famous Father

Despite his many connections to NASCAR, Dale Jr. did not spend much time at racetracks as a kid. His parents divorced in 1978, when he was four years old. He and Kelley lived with their mother until 1982, when their home was destroyed by a fire. Then the children moved in with their father and his new wife, Teresa Houston, in Mooresville, North Carolina. By this time Dale Sr. had worked his way up through NASCAR's racing divisions and won his first Winston Cup championship. His no-nonsense personality and aggressive driving style made him a fan favorite and earned him the nicknames The Intimidator and The Man in Black.

Dale Sr.'s racing career kept him extremely busy. He competed in races on more than 30 weekends per year and spent countless hours making public appearances on behalf of corporate sponsors. He also owned several Chevrolet dealerships and ran his own NASCAR race team, Dale Earnhardt Inc. (DEI). As a result, Dale Sr. did not spend much time with his children. "Dad was away racing most of the time," Dale Jr. remembered.

"He was so focused on winning that even when he was home between races, his mind was still at the racetrack instead of at home with us."

Although Dale Jr. admired his father and was proud of his racing success-es, he felt very distant from Dale Sr. through most of his youth. "[Dad] never really did anything with me. He never told me things. We were raised by six or seven nannies. I always thought he felt I wasn't much like him,"Dale Jr. recalled. "He was intimidating, like they say. He was like that as a father when he was at home.You wanted to please him all the time, make him happy, and you wanted to somehow get a response from him."

Dale Jr.'s mother, meanwhile, lived in Virginia and only managed to see the children on occasional weekends. "When she left, she'd cry,"he related. "It tore us up."With neither of his parents around much, Dale Jr. relied on his sister Kelley for emotional support. She defended him when he was teased by other kids who were jealous of their father's fame and wealth. "Kids bullied him,"Kelley acknowledged. "He was a lot smaller than they were. He was shy and sensitive and easily intimidated. He didn't stand up for himself. I never thought he'd race cars."

EDUCATION

By the time Dale Jr. reached his teen years, he had grown angry and re-sentful. He had trouble getting along with his stepmother and obeying his father's strict rules.They responded to his difficult behavior by sending him away to Oak Ridge Military Academy near Greensboro, North Carolina. Dale Jr. struggled to fit in at the school and was eventually kicked out. He returned home and graduated from Mooresville High School in 1992.

Since Dale Sr. had always placed a strong emphasis on education, Dale Jr. felt deeply disappointed when his father failed to attend his graduation ceremony. "Education.Yeah, it was such a big thing,"he said. "So I gradu-ated from high school, and where was my father? He didn't come to grad-uation. He was in a race somewhere. I understand now, of course, but I was looking forward to holding that diploma in his face. Except he wasn't there."Dale Jr. went on to earn an associate's degree in automotives from Mitchell Community College in Statesville, North Carolina.

CAREER HIGHLIGHTS

Breaking into Stock Car Racing

Earnhardt Jr. began to dabble in auto racing around the time he graduated from high school. He and his brother Kerry and sister Kelley bought a 1978 Chevrolet Monte Carlo at a junkyard, fixed it up, and took turns driving it in short-track races in NASCAR's Street Stock division. Their father never attended their races or offered them advice. Although Earnhardt Sr. had won four Winston Cup titles and earned millions of dollars in prize money by the time his children got involved in the sport, he did not think that they should receive any special treatment. He wanted them to work their way up through the ranks of NASCAR like other young drivers.

Earnhardt Jr. continued racing on weekends during college and afterward, while he worked as an auto mechanic and oil-change man at one of his father's Chevrolet dealerships in Newton, North Carolina. He learned a great deal about racing and steadily gained confidence as a driver. "I helped put together, work on, and set up my cars," he noted. "I learned from my mistakes. I wasn't a dominating driver, didn't win many races, but I was consistent."

Earnhardt Jr. impressed people in the racing industry with his talent and composure on the track. In 1994 Gary Hargett, a former driver and longtime friend of his father, offered him an opportunity to move up to the Late Model division. Earnhardt Jr. competed in 113 races over the next three seasons. Although he only chalked up three victories, he finished in the top 10 an impressive 90 times because he rarely crashed. His strong performance earned him several opportunities to compete in the Busch Series, which was considered NASCAR's training ground for future Winston Cup drivers. Earnhardt Jr. appeared in one Busch race in 1996 and eight more in 1997.

> — " —
>
> *Earnhardt Jr. revealed that gaining his father's attention was an important factor in his decision to race. "I wanted to impress him," he said. "I could have went and done other things, but no matter how successful I'd been … it wouldn't have been as impressive to him as winning a race."*
>
> — " —

Winning Back-to-Back Busch Series Titles

As Earnhardt Jr. worked his way up through the NASCAR divisions, Earnhardt Sr. gradually began to take notice of his son's abilities as a driver. Earnhardt Jr. acknowledged that gaining his father's attention was an important factor in his decision to race. "I wanted to impress him," he said. "I could have went and done other things, but no matter how successful I'd been … it wouldn't have been as impressive to him as winning a race."

*Earnhardt Jr. discussing preparation for a race with his father,
after Jr. joined Sr.'s race team, May 1998.*

As the start of the 1998 NASCAR race season approached, Dale Earnhardt Inc. had an opening for a Busch Series driver. The crew chief and many other members of the DEI race team encouraged Earnhardt Sr. to offer the job to his son. They argued that Earnhardt Jr. had earned a full-time ride in the Busch Series. Earnhardt Jr. drove the DEI car in pre-season test sessions, but weeks passed without Earnhardt Sr. making a decision. Earnhardt Jr. had almost given up on the idea when he accidentally learned that he would be driving for DEI in 1998. "I didn't know for sure that I was the driver until the name decals came into the shop two weeks before [the season-opening race at] Daytona," he recalled. "I know [my dad] just wants to teach me respect. He didn't want me to assume."

Earnhardt Jr. repaid his father's confidence in him by winning a race at Texas Motor Speedway on April 4, in only his 16th career Busch Series start. When he pulled his car into Victory Lane to accept his trophy, his father reacted with an uncharacteristic display of affection. Earnhardt Sr. rushed toward him, gave him a big hug, and told him how proud he was.

"It stirred memories of the years I had tried so hard to earn my dad's approval. Maybe that did it," Earnhardt Jr. remembered. "It really was a proud moment for him to show that much excitement and happiness over something that I had accomplished."

Earnhardt Jr. went on to win six more races in 1998. He thus earned enough points to claim the Busch Series championship in his first full season of competition on the circuit. (NASCAR drivers earn points based on their finishing position in races, number of laps led, number of pole positions earned, and other criteria. At the end of each season, the drivers who earn the most points in their division are named champions.) Earnhardt Jr. became the first third-generation driver to win the Busch Series points title, following in the footsteps of his father and grandfather. At the conclusion of his highly successful first season with DEI, Earnhardt Jr. signed a five-year sponsorship deal with Budweiser worth $50 million.

As the 1999 season got underway, Earnhardt Jr. emerged as the most popular driver in the Busch Series. NASCAR fans not only recognized his famous name, but they also liked his red number 3 Budweiser Chevrolet and his hard-charging driving style. "I enjoy that kind of racing, hate watching a race that looks like a bunch of toy soldiers marching around," Earnhardt Jr. explained. "Fans like action, even if their favorite driver gets bumped around or spun out." He rewarded fans for their support by claiming six race victories and a second consecutive Busch Series championship. He also appeared in five Winston Cup Series races during the 1999 season, posting a best finishing position of tenth.

Moving Up to Winston Cup

On the strength of his back-to-back titles in the Busch Series, Earnhardt Jr. earned the opportunity to compete in the prestigious Winston Cup Series full-time in 2000. Since his father championed the number 3 in Winston Cup, Earnhardt Jr. chose the number 8, which had once belonged to his grandfather. In the season-opening Daytona 500—the biggest race of the NASCAR season, held in February each year—he finished a respectable 13th and beat his father for the first time. On April 2 Earnhardt Jr. claimed his first victory, at Texas Motor Speedway, in only his 12th career Winston Cup race. "It was fun to get out front and show these guys I could use my head and make smart decisions," he said afterward.

Only a month later, Earnhardt Jr. claimed a second victory at Richmond International Speedway, crossing the finish line only 0.159 seconds ahead of veteran driver Terry Labonte. "We are the first team to take two races this season," he noted. "Rookie team, rookie driver. Winners, not just once, but

*The 2001 Daytona 500, with Jr. in the #8 Budweiser Chevy
and Sr. in the #3 Goodwrench Chevy.*

twice." On the strength of his two wins, Earnhardt Jr. earned enough points to finish 16th in the Winston Cup standings at the end of the season. He narrowly missed winning the Raybestos Rookie of the Year Award, finishing 42 points behind fellow rookie driver Matt Kenseth.

One of the things Earnhardt Jr. enjoyed most about his rookie Winston Cup season, however, was that it brought him closer to his father. Being involved in NASCAR's highest level of racing gave Earnhardt Jr. a new understanding of the pressures and demands that his father had long faced. It also enabled the two men to hang out together at the track and relate to each other as friends and colleagues. Several longtime Winston Cup drivers remarked that the presence of his son seemed to rekindle Earnhardt Sr.'s interest in racing. "It totally changed Dale Sr.'s outlook on things," said racer Dave Marcis. "He became more competitive and rejuvenated."

Dealing with Tragedy

Following his strong rookie year, Earnhardt Jr. eagerly anticipated the start of the 2001 Winston Cup season. As always, the season opened with the biggest race on the NASCAR schedule, the Daytona 500. Earnhardt Jr.'s car ran well throughout the race. With only a few laps to go, he found himself running second behind his DEI teammate, Michael Waltrip, with his father sitting behind him in third place.

Earnhardt Sr. did not seem to have enough power to pass his son or Waltrip, so he tried to prevent other cars from getting by him in order to ensure victory for a member of his race team. His strategy worked, as Waltrip streaked across the finish line to take the checkered flag, followed closely by Earnhardt Jr. in second. As Earnhardt Sr. entered the final turn, however, his car was bumped from behind by fellow driver Sterling Marlin. Earnhardt Sr. lost control of the car and crashed into the concrete barrier on the outside of the track at 180 miles per hour. Although the crash did not initially appear to be life-threatening, NASCAR fans soon learned that Earnhardt Sr. had died instantly from severe head and neck injuries.

The tragic loss of the NASCAR legend shocked and saddened race fans everywhere. Makeshift memorials to Earnhardt Sr. appeared at racetracks across the country, and thousands of people displayed his number 3 on T-shirts, flags, banners, and window stickers. Earnhardt Jr. took the news of his father's death very hard. He struggled to find a way to come to terms with his grief. "I lost the greatest man I ever knew," he stated. "I miss my father, and I've cried for him. I'm trying to maintain a good focus for the future and just remember that he's in a better place, a place we all want to be…. We'll get through this. I'm sure he'd want us to keep going, and that's what we're going to do."

Although Earnhardt Jr. returned to competition the following week, he did poorly over the next few races. He finally broke through for his first victory of the season on July 7, when the Winston Cup Series returned to Daytona for the first time since Earnhardt Sr.'s death. Earnhardt Jr. turned in one of the best performances of his career, leading 116 of 160 laps and fighting his way back from sixth to first with only a few laps remaining. Waltrip, his DEI teammate who had won the Daytona 500, finished second. Earnhardt Jr. claimed that he had felt his father's presence throughout the race. "He was with me," he declared. "I know I did it, but he was there."

Earnhardt Jr. went on to win two more races in the 2001 season, giving him 15 finishes in the top 10 and placing him eighth in the Winston Cup point standings. During the off-season he published a book called *Driver #8*. It describes what it was like growing up as the son of a famous driver, provides a race-by-race chronicle of his rookie season of Winston Cup competition, and concludes with the tragic death of his father. NASCAR fans snapped up copies of the memoir, vaulting it onto the *New York Times* best-seller list. Earnhardt Jr. also joined his stepmother, Teresa, as part-owner of a Busch Series race team called Chance 2 Motorsports. Chance 2 hired a young driver, Martin Truex Jr., who went on to win back-to-back Busch Series championships in 2004 and 2005.

Winning the 2004 Daytona 500

In the 2002 Winston Cup season, Earnhardt Jr. won two races and posted six finishes in the top 10. These results were good enough to claim 11th place in the Winston Cup point standings. Earnhardt Jr. performed more consistently in 2003, winning two races and finishing in the top 10 a career-high 21 times. His strong performance lifted him to an impressive third in the season-ending point standings—the best finish of his career. At the end of the year he was thrilled to receive the NASCAR Most Popular Driver Award from the National Motorsports Press Association.

Prior to the start of the 2004 season, NASCAR introduced a number of changes. It dropped Winston cigarettes as the sponsor of its premier race series in favor of the telecommunications company Nextel, so the Winston Cup became the Nextel Cup. It also created a 10-race playoff system called the Chase for the Cup in an effort to tighten competition and increase fan interest toward the end of the season. Only the 12 drivers ranked highest in the point standings with 10 races remaining would qualify for the Chase and compete for the championship.

As always, though, the 2004 NASCAR season started with the Daytona 500. Earnhardt Jr. made it his personal mission to win the prestigious race as a way to honor his father's legacy. He led the first 29 laps and ran near the front all day. Toward the end of the race, it became clear that the two strongest cars belonged to Earnhardt Jr. and Tony Stewart. Earnhardt Jr. made a daring pass of Stewart with a few laps remaining to clinch the victory. "Every time we come to Daytona, it feels like I'm closer to Dad. But at the same time it's a reminder of losing him. So I wanted to come down here and win," he said afterward. "This is like you can't write a better script.... It's just the greatest race. It's the greatest day of my life. I really can't describe it."

Winning the Daytona 500 turned out to be the beginning of an outstanding season for Earnhardt Jr. He won a total of 6 races that year and posted 21 finishes in the top 10, which easily allowed him to qualify for the inaugural Chase. He actually led the standings briefly with seven races left, but he dropped to second when NASCAR officials penalized him 25 points for swearing in a post-race TV interview. The controversial decision turned out to be a key turning point in his season, and he ended up finishing fifth in the point standings. Still, he won the Most Popular Driver Award for the second straight year.

Earnhardt Jr. celebrating his win at the 2004 Daytona 500.

By the time Earnhardt Jr. completed his fourth full Cup season, he had become one of the most marketable athletes in the United States. NASCAR fans appreciated his good looks, down-to-earth personality, casual style, and hip interests. But his popularity extended well beyond the traditional stock car racing fan base, making him one of the first true crossover stars in NASCAR history. In fact, some observers described him as the "face of NASCAR" because he helped expand interest in the sport nationwide. Earnhardt Jr.'s appeal led to a number of business and endorsement opportunities. He gave an interview on the national TV news show "60 Minutes," hosted his own auto racing shows on cable TV, served as a presenter at the annual Country Music Awards, and developed racing video games. Although he enjoyed some aspects of his fame, Earnhardt Jr. also admitted that he sometimes wished he had more personal privacy and fewer demands on his time.

Leaving His Father's Race Team

The 2005 Nextel Cup season was a disappointing one for Earnhardt Jr. He earned only one victory and 13 top-10 finishes, failed to qualify for the

Earnhardt Jr. with the Hendrick Motorsports team. From left:
driver Jimmie Johnson; driver Todd Bodine; team owner Rick Hendrick;
driver Mark Martin; driver Jeff Gordon; and Earnhardt Jr.

Chase, and ended up 19th in the point standings. He performed more consistently during the 2006 season, posting his 17th career victory and earning 17 finishes in the top 10. Although his results were good enough to qualify for the Chase, he only managed to finish fifth in the point standings. He remained a favorite among NASCAR fans, however, and claimed the Most Popular Driver Award in both 2005 and 2006.

As the 2007 Nextel Cup season approached, NASCAR observers noted that Earnhardt Jr.'s contract with DEI was due to expire at the end of the year. Teresa Earnhardt had taken ownership of her husband's race team following Earnhardt Sr.'s death in 2001. Since then, Earnhardt Jr. and his stepmother had disagreed publicly about the future direction of DEI on several occasions. Teresa also claimed that Earnhardt Jr.'s popularity and outside interests distracted him from his job as a driver.

Earnhardt Jr., on the other hand, blamed the team owner and DEI management for not spending the money necessary to build elite race cars. He argued that DEI could not be a top-notch race team with non-racers in charge of the business. He tried to buy a controlling interest in his father's company, but his stepmother refused to consider his offer. Despite the high-profile differences of opinion, however, most observers felt confident that the two sides would eventually iron out their problems so that Earnhardt Jr. could remain with DEI.

During the 2007 Nextel Cup season, however, Earnhardt Jr. failed to win a race for the first time in his career, did not finish a career-high nine races, missed qualifying for the Chase, and ended up a disappointing 16th in the point standings. Midway through the frustrating season, Earnhardt Jr. shocked many NASCAR fans by announcing his decision to leave DEI at the end of 2007. "I had to leave and get out and do my own thing," he declared. "It's time for me to take charge of my career. It's time for me to start winning championships."

A month after announcing his departure from DEI, Earnhardt Jr. shocked NASCAR fans once again by signing a contract with rival Hendrick Motorsports (HMS). HMS was the most dominant team in Nextel Cup competition. Its talented stable of drivers included four-time champion Jeff Gordon and two-time defending champion Jimmie Johnson. HMS drivers had won fully half of the 36 races on the Nextel Cup schedule in 2007. Many fans of Earnhardt Jr. and his father, however, had long viewed Hendrick Motorsports as the bitter enemy of their favorite drivers. They especially disliked the young, clean-cut, California-born Gordon, whom they felt had prevented Earnhardt Sr. from capturing a record eighth career Winston Cup title in the late 1990s.

Earnhardt Jr. joined rival team Hendrick Motorsports to become more competitive. "I'm a racer, and I just want to win races and contend for championships. Now that I'm with Rick [Hendrick], that's going to start happening," he stated. "I understand that I have no more excuses. Now I'll have the best equipment and the best people behind me. It's time for me to start winning."

Still, Earnhardt Jr. found the idea of driving for HMS very appealing. He felt comfortable with the team owner, Rick Hendrick, whom he had known for many years as a friend and competitor of his father. "He's kind of like a father figure to me and has been for a long time," he noted. Earnhardt Jr. also appreciated Hendrick's state-of-the-art race shop and technology-driven approach to racing. He believed that gaining access to HMS equipment and engineers would make him more competitive. "I'm a racer, and I just want to win races and contend for championships. Now that I'm with Rick, that's going to start happening," he stated. "I understand that I have no more excuses. Now I'll have the best equipment and the best people behind me. It's time for me to start winning."

Seeking a Championship

In addition to switching teams, Earnhardt Jr.'s racing effort underwent a number of other changes prior to the start of the 2008 season. His primary sponsor changed from Budweiser to Mountain Dew/Amp Energy Drink and the U.S. National Guard. In addition, the color of his car changed from red to green, and his number changed from 8 to 88. Since NASCAR fans purchase millions of dollars worth of merchandise every year bearing the name and number of their favorite drivers, all of these changes forced Earnhardt Jr.'s many fans to overhaul their wardrobes. NASCAR underwent a change in 2008 as well, as the Nextel Cup became the Sprint Cup.

All of the changes appeared to be positive for Earnhardt Jr. as the 2008 Sprint Cup season got underway. He won the first two races he competed in for HMS, the Bud Shootout exhibition race and the Gatorade Duel qualifying race, which are held as part of the festivities surrounding the Daytona 500 but do not count toward the Sprint Cup point standings. He finished ninth in the big race that weekend, then went on to finish in the top 10 in three of the next four races. Earnhardt Jr. notched the 18th race victory of his 10-year Cup career at Michigan International Speedway on Father's Day. "It's special—my daddy meant a lot to me," he said afterward. "I know I can't tell my father 'Happy Father's Day,' but I get to wish all fathers a happy day. I mean it." His one victory and 16 top-10 finishes enabled him to qualify for the Chase, but he ended up 12th in the final point standings. He still won his sixth consecutive Most Popular Driver Award, while his HMS teammate Johnson claimed his third straight Sprint Cup title.

Earnhardt Jr. hoped to improve his results in 2009, but he struggled throughout his second season with HMS. He was assigned a new crew chief, Lance McGrew, to replace his cousin, Tony Eury Jr. Eury Jr. had moved from DEI to Hendrick along with Earnhardt Jr., but he had trouble fitting into the disciplined, high-tech atmosphere at HMS. As Earnhardt Jr. and McGrew tried to establish a good working relationship, the 88 car's performance on the track suffered. Earnhardt Jr. failed to win a race for only the second time in his Cup career, posted only five top-10 finishes, and finished a career-worst 25th in the point standings. Meanwhile, Johnson won a fourth consecutive Sprint Cup championship, and two other HMS drivers (Mark Martin and Gordon) finished second and third in the points. "Maybe Junior has struggled a little to adapt to the culture of Hen-

Earnhardt Jr. in #88 comes in for a pit stop during a race.

drick,"Johnson said. "It's a demanding place, and if you're not totally committed, you might struggle."

Earnhardt Jr. took a break at the end of the 2009 season to recharge his batteries, and he came back in 2010 with an improved attitude. "This was the best off-season of my life because it was the first time I can remember that I got away from the sport," he explained. "I just stayed at home and remembered that I've won races, a lot of big trophies, and that I know how to drive these cars. My confidence came back." Earnhardt Jr. demonstrated his newfound confidence at the Daytona 500. In what some observers described as the best driving of his life, he passed eight cars in the final two laps to finish in second place. "It was a blur," he said afterward. "I just held the gas pedal down and prayed."

Unfortunately, Earnhardt Jr.'s struggles continued later in the 2010 season. He went winless for the second straight year, only managed to finish in the top 10 eight times, failed to qualify for the Chase, and ended up 21st in the point standings. His teammate Johnson had another great year and claimed his fifth straight Sprint Cup title, while Earnhardt Jr. won the Most Popular Driver Award for the eighth time.

In 2011 Earnhardt Jr. changed crew chiefs again and began working with Steve Letarte, who had formerly been Gordon's crew chief. "Confidence breeds confidence," Letarte stated. "I know he can drive, I know he can win, I know our cars can win, and I'm excited to give him a platform week in and week out that he can display his talents."Rick Hendrick also moved the 88 car into the same race shop as Johnson's 48 team, in hopes that Earnhardt Jr.'s crew might benefit from knowing the five-time champion's strategy and setup.

The changes seemed to help, as Earnhardt Jr. ran well through much of the 2011 season. Although he did not win a race, he came close on several occasions. He was poised to win the Coca-Cola 600 at Charlotte Motor Speedway in May, for instance, until his car ran out of gas in the final turn. He ended up with 11 finishes in the top 10, qualified for the Chase, and finished ninth in the point standings. In accepting the Most Popular Driver Award for the ninth consecutive year, Earnhardt Jr. expressed satisfaction with the improvement in his results and optimism about his chances for 2012. "I'm happy to be competing again and I feel like I'm almost where I want to be," he said. "This year it turned all around, 180 degrees, and I'm enjoying it again and I didn't want the season to come to an end…. I feel much more excited about my future."

Dealing with High Expectations

The 2011 Sprint Cup season was Earnhardt Jr.'s best since joining Hendrick Motorsports, but most observers feel that he has not lived up to the high expectations that accompanied his move. After all, Earnhardt Jr. enjoys access to the same engineering expertise and well-prepared cars as Johnson and the other HMS drivers, yet he has only produced one victory and has never contended for the Cup championship in four seasons. By the end of 2011, his winless streak extended to more than 120 races. Although he remains a huge favorite among NASCAR fans, critics claim that his on-track performance does not support his popularity.

Few people question that Earnhardt Jr. has talent as a driver, but some people wonder whether he possesses the dedication and focus necessary to compete at the highest level. "It was eye-opening for Dale, the level of intensity at HMS," said Gordon. "How hard everyone works. Jimmie [Johnson] works out at a gym five times a week. He pays attention to details."Earnhardt Jr. acknowledges that he does not maintain as rigorous a training schedule as some other NASCAR drivers. "I try to keep in shape, eat right, lift weights. But I don't do it all the time," he admitted. "Jimmie hardly ever makes a step without thinking how it's gonna affect his racing. But I don't believe in living like that. I'd have to become a different person. I'm not willing to devote that much to it."

Other observers claim that the problem lies not with Earnhardt Jr., but with the unreasonably high expectations he has faced throughout his career as the son of a legendary seven-time Cup champion. "Dale Jr. has never gotten a fair shake from the start because, guess what, he's not his father," said fellow driver Kevin Harvick. "He was always supposed to have been someone else. The pressure he's under is unreal." Even though he has not captured a title of his own, Earnhardt Jr. has accumulated a respectable 18 Cup wins and $58 million in race earnings in 10 full seasons on the circuit. In addition, he has accomplished these things while facing more intense fan pressure and media scrutiny than any other driver.

Earnhardt Jr. recognizes that living up to his father's legacy is a difficult task. "I still love racing, still love the challenge. I really want to win a championship one day, but if that never happens, I'll still be happy," he stated. "You know, I never thought I'd accomplish everything that I have in racing. I may have this name, but I never thought of myself being like my father. He was just so big, man, larger than life. It's a damn tough act to follow."

Earnhardt Jr. has acknowledged that living up to his father's legacy is a difficult task. "I still love racing, still love the challenge. I really want to win a championship one day, but if that never happens, I'll still be happy," he stated. "You know, I never thought I'd accomplish everything that I have in racing. I may have this name, but I never thought of myself being like my father. He was just so big, man, larger than life. It's a damn tough act to follow."

HOME AND FAMILY

Earnhardt Jr. lives on 140 acres of land near Mooresville, North Carolina. His property features a six-hole golf course, three go-kart tracks, a regulation boxing ring, and a replica Western frontier town with a saloon, a hotel, and a jail. He shares his home with a variety of pets, including dogs, cats, and a pair of bison.

Earnhardt Jr. has never been married, and he has always kept his personal relationships strictly private. In late 2011, however, he introduced his girlfriend Amy Reimann to the media after dating her for more than a year.

Nine-time Most Popular Driver winner Earnhardt Jr. signing autographs for fans.

HOBBIES AND OTHER INTERESTS

In his spare time, Earnhardt Jr. enjoys hanging out at home, playing video games, and tinkering with computers. He also maintains a wide variety of business and charitable interests. He owns a Nationwide race team called JR Motorsports, which signed Danica Patrick to its roster of drivers in 2010. He also owns a bar and nightclub called Whisky River in Charlotte. In 2007 he launched the Dale Jr. Foundation to help underprivileged youth gain confidence through education. The foundation lends support to 700 local and national youth organizations. Finally, Earnhardt Jr. is active with the Make-a-Wish Foundation.

HONORS AND AWARDS

Busch (Nationwide) Series Champion: 1998, 1999
NASCAR Most Popular Driver (National Motorsports Press Association): 2003-2011

FURTHER READING

Books

Earnhardt, Dale Jr., with Jade Gurss. *Driver #8,* 2002

Hillstrom, Laurie Collier. *People in the News: Dale Earnhardt Jr.,* 2009 (juvenile)

MacDonald, James. *Dale Earnhardt, Jr.: Racing's Living Legacy,* 2008 (juvenile)

Periodicals

Current Biography Yearbook, 2007
New York Times, Jan. 20, 2008, p.3
New York Times Magazine, Aug. 8, 2010, p.22
Sporting News, August 6, 2001, p.48; Feb. 14, 2011, p.48
Sports Illustrated, July 1, 2002, p.60; May 26, 2004, p.12; Dec. 5, 2007; Feb. 18, 2008, p.72; Nov. 25, 2010, p.62

Online Articles

www.notablebiographies.com/news/Ca-Ge/Earnhardt-Dale-Jr.html
(Encyclopedia of World Biography, "Dale Earnhardt Jr. Biography," no date)
espn.go.com/racing
(ESPN, "Dale Earnhardt Jr., multiple articles, various dates)
espn.go.com/racing/nascar/cup/story/_/id/7525221
(ESPN, "Dale Earnhardt Jr.'s Confidence Surging," Feb. 7, 2012)
topics.nytimes.com/pages/topics
(New York Times, "Dale Earnhardt Jr.," multiple articles, various dates)
sportsillustrated.cnn.com
(Sports Illustrated, "Dale Earnhardt Jr.: A Junior Renaissance," Jan. 12, 2012)

ADDRESS

Dale Earnhardt Jr.
Hendrick Motorsports
4400 Papa Joe Hendrick Blvd.
Charlotte, NC 28262

WEB SITES

www.dalejr.com
www.nascar.com
www.hendrickmotorsports.com

Heidi Hammel 1960-

American Scientist and Planetary Astronomer
Pioneering Researcher in Astronomical Observation
of the Planets Neptune and Uranus

BIRTH

Heidi Hammel was born on March 14, 1960, in Sacramento, California. Her father, Bob, worked a variety of different jobs, and her mother, Phyllis, was a homemaker and former nurse. Hammel has an older brother named Hazen and a younger sister named Lisa.

YOUTH

Hammel's family moved around a lot when she was young, moving to a new location whenever her father changed jobs.

By the time Hammel was six years old, her family had lived in five homes in three different cities in California. They relocated to Pennsylvania and moved two more times before finally settling in Clarks Summit, Pennsylvania, in 1970, when she was ten years old.

No matter where the family lived, their house was always full of books and magazines. Hammel loved to read, especially science fiction stories. She was a fan of the television show "Star Trek" and spent hours studying blueprints of the "Star Trek" spaceship, Enterprise. She liked to climb trees and go exploring with her brother. She took swimming lessons and piano lessons, built things with Lego blocks, and loved music and singing in the church choir. Her parents encouraged her creativity and imagination and provided plenty of opportunities for Hammel to learn new things. Family vacations were spent visiting museums and other places that taught about nature, history, or culture. One of her favorite things to do was to invent new games to play with her best friend. She would combine different card games to create a new game, like putting three or four Monopoly sets together with the Game of Life, or figuring out how to play Gin Rummy with five decks of cards.

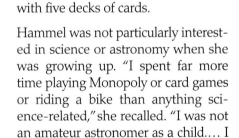

"I used to get car sick, and my parents used to take us on trips a lot in the car and so I had to lie on the back seat being sick, and the only thing I could do was look out the window and see the stars. And so I learned the constellations, I learned what the bright stars were, and so that's what kept me going on those long car trips."

Hammel was not particularly interested in science or astronomy when she was growing up. "I spent far more time playing Monopoly or card games or riding a bike than anything science-related," she recalled. "I was not an amateur astronomer as a child.... I used to get car sick, and my parents used to take us on trips a lot in the car and so I had to lie on the back seat being sick, and the only thing I could do was look out the window and see the stars. And so I learned the constellations, I learned what the bright stars were, and so that's what kept me going on those long car trips."

"The second thing I remember, when I was a kid, is going to a planetarium, and they would do a star show about what the stars were looking like and what was 'up'—the planets—and that was all kind of boring, but then at some point during the show a comet would streak across the sky with flames and a roar that was really loud, and you never knew when it was going to happen, and it was really exciting. And I would go back to the planetarium again and again and again just to wait for that comet to come. And I think I probably picked up a little astronomy along the way when I was doing that."

Hammel's parents divorced when she was in middle school. After that, she lived with her mother, brother, and sister, and saw her father occasionally.

EDUCATION

Hammel went to Abington Heights Middle School and Abington Heights High School in Clarks Summit, Pennsylvania. She was good at math and enjoyed science classes. She was a member of the school band and played percussion instruments, including drums, xylophone, and chimes. She also liked to sing and act, and she performed in school plays. She was a good student who usually got high grades in all of her classes. Hammel graduated from high school in 1978.

After high school, Hammel began studying at the Massachusetts Institute of Technology (MIT) in Cambridge, Massachusetts. A research university that focuses on science and technology, MIT is one of the premier universities in the United States—and one of the most difficult. Though Hammel had always done well in her courses in high school, she found her classes at MIT to be extremely challenging. "MIT was just an awful, awful experience for me. You get to MIT and you work and work and work and then you fail. And work-work-work harder, and you fail," she recalled. "I struggled so hard. Nobody seemed to be working as hard as I did and they were getting much better grades. I was not a very happy person there. I learned how to work hard and how to cope with failure. I learned you couldn't let things get you down. If you persevere, the rewards will come later on." Hammel was committed to succeeding at MIT and managed to pass her freshman year.

In her sophomore year, Hammel impulsively decided to take an observational astronomy course. Observational astronomy is the study of space and objects such as planets, stars, and galaxies through the use of telescopes and other scientific devices. Though she knew nothing about astronomy, she thought the course sounded like fun. The coursework turned out to be very difficult and Hammel considered dropping out of the class. She decided to finish the course with the encouragement and support of her professor. By the end of that semester, she had decided to major in astronomy.

As she continued in the astronomy program, Hammel quickly found that she had a natural talent for understanding the data she gathered in her research. She also discovered a talent for creative problem-solving. If her research data was not exactly what she needed, she would come up with

Hammel shown with images taken with a space telescope.

ways to improve the performance of her research equipment. For example, Hammel found that the telescope she was using was not producing images that were clear enough for her work. She made a tube that fit on the end of the telescope to block out the stray light that was making her images blurry. She also created a special filter that allowed the telescope to detect more kinds of light, helping her to gather even more information about the stars and planets she was observing.

Though Hammel continued to work hard in her classes, she did not limit her time at MIT to just studying. She joined MIT's musical theater guild and played percussion in the orchestra that accompanied theater performances. She also sang in a local church choir and had a part-time job playing guitar in a bluegrass band that performed in a coffee shop in MIT's student center.

In 1982, Hammel earned a Bachelor of Science degree (BS) in Earth and Planetary Science from MIT. She immediately enrolled in graduate school at the University of Hawaii, planning to earn her doctorate, or PhD.

An advanced degree in astronomy requires courses in math, statistics, data analysis, and physics. Hammel had a talent for working with data and numbers, but she found the physics classes to be extremely difficult. After her first two years at the University of Hawaii, she needed to pass qualifying exams in order to continue in the graduate program. These tests included an extensive oral exam, during which a panel of professors could ask her about any aspect of astronomy. Hammel did not pass the qualifying oral exam the first time she took it. The doctoral committee gave her an opportunity to retake the oral exam, and she passed the test on her second try.

Passing the qualifying exam meant that Hammel would be allowed to finish her graduate degree. To do this, she needed to complete a new, original research project. Though she didn't know it at the time, the research she chose to conduct would mark the beginning of her career as a pioneer of astronomy.

CAREER HIGHLIGHTS

The Ice Giants

Hammel's astronomy career actually began while she was still in graduate school. For her doctoral research project, she decided to study the planets Uranus and Neptune. These are the two planets in the solar system that are located the farthest away from Earth. They are known as Ice Giants. Ice Giants are massive planets with atmospheres made of various types of gases that are poisonous to humans. Ice Giants are believed to have slushy surfaces and icy or semi-molten rocky cores. Many details of the nature and composition of Ice Giants are unknown because of their remote location and inhospitable atmospheres.

Hammel's graduate research project included the use of astronomical imaging to study the atmospheres of Uranus and Neptune. Astronomical imaging uses special telescopes equipped with filters that can separate the different types of light waves that reflect off of a planet, to make images that show each type of light individually. This kind of information helps astronomers to determine the elements or materials that make up a planet, because each element or material reflects light in a different way.

In her research, Hammel wanted to learn about the clouds, winds, and weather on the two planets, and how these things changed over time. She knew that up to that time, no one had studied Uranus and Neptune in this way. No matter what she discovered in her research, all of it would be new information. She would be a pioneer in this area of astronomy.

"One thing that we all care about is the weather," Hammel explained. "And we care about the weather on the Earth the most. But what makes weather is gases and clouds. And the reason the weather on the Earth is hard to predict is because we have oceans and continents that interact with our atmosphere. That makes it very hard to predict the weather, as we all know. But if you take a planet like Jupiter or Neptune, you don't have continents and you don't have oceans. All you have is gas. All you have is atmosphere. And therefore it is a lot easier to model the weather on those planets. But it's the same physical process, it's the same kind of thing happening whether it happens on the Earth or whether it happens on Neptune. Therefore, by studying weather on Neptune we learn about weather in general, and that helps us understand the weather on Earth better."

Hammel began her research by collecting images of Uranus using a huge, powerful telescope owned by the University of Hawaii. This telescope was located at the top of Mauna Kea. As the tallest mountain in Hawaii, Mauna Kea stands more than 13,000 feet above sea level. At this extremely high altitude, the thin, dry air can cause headaches and drowsiness, and the increased atmospheric pressure can make people feel nauseous. But that same thin air provides an ideal environment for astronomical observation. Mauna Kea is considered one of the best sites in the world for astronomers, and demand for telescope time there is high. Astronomers often get to use the telescope for only a few hours at a time to make their observations.

The images Hammel collected at Mauna Kea provided a wealth of new information about Uranus. As she analyzed the data from her images, she gained a better understanding of the planet's cloud patterns, weather systems, wind speeds and directions, and how all of these changed over time. But there was only so much data that Hammel could gather with a telescope located on the ground. In order to learn more, she would need to see data collected closer to the distant planet.

In 1986, Hammel got a unique opportunity to do just that. She was among a group of young scientists who were invited by NASA to study close-up

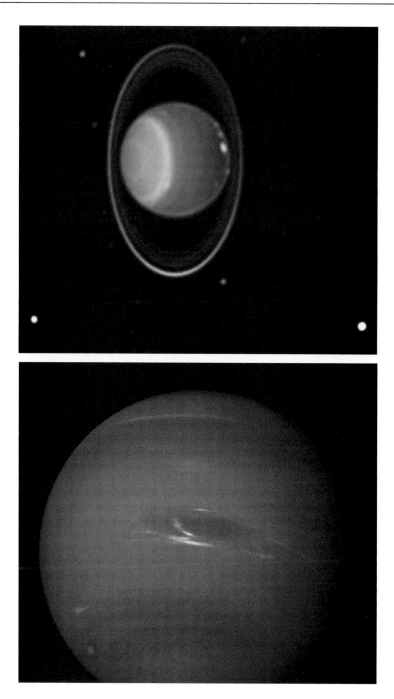

*Photos of Uranus and Neptune, the Ice Giants
that Hammel has spent years studying.*

images of Uranus as they were transmitted back to Earth by the Voyager 2 spacecraft. The mission of Voyager 2, which was launched in 1977, was to explore the farthest reaches of the solar system and send information about deep space back to Earth. By 1986 Voyager 2 had reached Uranus, and it collected a series of images and other data as it flew by. Hammel was excited at the chance to be among the first to see what Voyager 2 had found.

Voyager 2 collected a huge amount of previously unknown information about Uranus. The data and images provided new insight on Uranus's moons, rings, and magnetic field. But there was very little information about the atmosphere of Uranus. Though she could appreciate the importance of the other data, Hammel was disappointed at the lack of atmospheric information.

Becoming an Expert

As Voyager 2 continued on its exploration, it left Uranus and headed towards Neptune. The data it collected about Neptune was expected to reach Earth in three years. Hammel hoped that Voyager 2 would provide more substantial data about Neptune's atmosphere, which was very difficult to observe using telescopes on Earth. While she waited to see what Voyager 2 discovered about Neptune, Hammel decided to focus her own astronomical observations on that planet. She wanted to learn as much as she could about Neptune so that she would be prepared to analyze the data from Voyager 2.

Hammel began collecting images of Neptune using the big telescope on Mauna Kea. To her surprise, her images looked nothing like those taken by other astronomers in previous years. Her images showed that Neptune's atmosphere looked completely different than it had a short time before. Well-known astronomers said that Hammel must have done something wrong to get such radically different images. The controversy grew when she published more of her findings that included data showing that Neptune was rotating faster than previously believed. Hammel defended her work and was eventually able to persuade her critics that she was right.

Throughout this time, Hammel had been a graduate student at the University of Hawaii. In 1988, she received her PhD in physics and astronomy from the University of Hawaii. In 1989, she accepted a post-doctoral position with NASA's Jet Propulsion Laboratory team. This group was working with Voyager 2, and Hammel would be part of the mission team when the spacecraft flew by Neptune. By the time she was 29 years old, she was widely regarded as the expert on Neptune.

Once Voyager 2 began transmitting data about Neptune, Hammel understood why so little had been known about the planet before. As she ana-

A photo of the Hubble Space Telescope drifting over the Earth.

lyzed the data and compared it to images she collected with the Mauna Kea telescope, she saw two very different pictures of the same planet. Voyager 2 provided the first images of Neptune's Great Dark Spot, which could not be seen by telescopes on Earth. Hammel combined the data from her telescope observations with the Voyager 2 data, and for the first time a complete picture of Neptune's atmosphere came into view. Her work provided a new understanding of Neptune's weather, which would help scientists better understand the Earth's weather patterns.

In 1990, Hammel became the Principal Research Scientist in MIT's Department of Earth, Atmospheric and Planetary Sciences. This position allowed her to continue collecting information about Neptune and other giant planets. It also put her in the right place, at the right time, to lead the team that would observe one of the most important astronomical events of her generation—the Great Comet Crash of 1994.

The Great Comet Crash

During the week of July 16-22, 1994, a comet named Shoemaker-Levy 9 was expected to crash into Jupiter, the largest planet in the solar system. Shoemaker-Levy 9 consisted of a string of 21 smaller pieces that had been circling Jupiter on a collision course for some time. This event was highly anticipated by astronomers around the world because it was such a rare occurrence. It would be the first time that people could observe the collision of two planetary bodies and study the impact of such a collision.

"Events like these were critical to the formation and evolution of the planets, and this was the first time astronomers had a chance to observe such an encounter," Hammel explained. Her team would use the Hubble Space Telescope to collect images and data as the crash happened. The Hubble Space Telescope is located in space above Earth's atmosphere, where it can capture images with less distortion than ground telescopes. It's been orbiting around the Earth since 1990, when it was ferried into orbit by a space shuttle.

> "I ran into an amateur astronomer who had a small telescope set up on the sidewalk. I looked through the lens at Jupiter, and I saw the explosions [from the Great Comet Crash]. Something was happening 500 million miles away and I was staring at it on a street corner in Baltimore," Hammel said. "When I saw those black spots, it hit me right in the gut. This wasn't something just for astronomers. It belonged to everyone."

"I just love working with Hubble.... It's incredible to me that there is a robotic telescope in orbit around the Earth, and that you can design a program and send these sequences up and move this telescope around to point anywhere around the sky and do any kind of science and get absolutely fabulous pictures, without the Earth's atmosphere in the way. You just can't do this from the ground," Hammel explained. "But with Hubble you only get one chance, so you've got to do it right the first time. That means you have to work very, very hard to make sure you have everything completely understood and you can't take chances and that makes it hard to use."

Hammel's challenge in preparing the Hubble Space Telescope to observe the Great Comet Crash was that no one knew what to expect, or how to prepare for observing and recording the event. She needed to figure out where to point the Hubble Space Telescope, which filters to use, when to take pictures, and many other details. Without really knowing what the collision would entail, Hammel began making calculations based on her best guesses of what would happen.

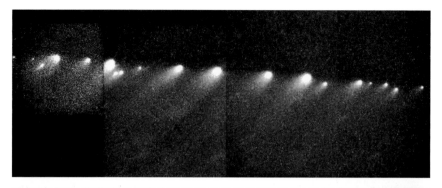

Two images related to the Great Comet Crash: the Shoemaker-Levy 9 comet in space (top) and the impact sites on Jupiter after the crash (bottom). The image of the comet is actually multiple photos pieced together.

Hammel guessed correctly, and her calculations produced more than 400 images from the Hubble Space Telescope of the Great Comet Crash. The images were clear and richly detailed, providing a huge amount of surprising new data. As the team leader, Hammel presented the first images to the world, exclaiming, "In my wildest dreams we couldn't have gotten any better!" Speaking to members of the press from around the world, she became the public face of the team working on the Great Comet Crash. Her excitement and enthusiasm were contagious, and her ability to explain complex astronomical observations in plain language helped non-scientists understand the significance of the collision.

"There's a little bit more to it than just the science," Hammel explained. "Of course, we're interested in science here because that's what we do. But it's a fascinating thing. There are things whizzing around the solar system, smashing into other things with huge explosions, and that's just really incredible to think about. We don't often think about the universe out there. We just sort of look at the sky and stars up there and—big deal. But if we really take a step back, it's a dynamic universe. And this is just a key example of some of the energetics that go on." She continued by explaining the powerful impact of the collision. "It made plumes of gases that rose 1,000 miles high. Jupiter was covered with atmospheric soot. If that impact had happened on Earth, we all would have died. It would have created a major disruption of the biosphere. This is what we think happened to the dinosaurs."

The Great Comet Crash fascinated the entire astronomy community, including amateurs who were able to observe the collision even with their small telescopes. "I ran into an amateur astronomer who had a small telescope set up on the sidewalk. I looked through the lens at Jupiter, and I saw the explosions. Something was happening 500 million miles away and I was staring at it on a street corner in Baltimore. I got a hitch in my chest. I was just amazed," Hammel recalled. "It was just an incredible sight. I had spent months planning the whole thing with Hubble. But I had never physically looked through an eyepiece to see what was happening. When I saw those black spots, it hit me right in the gut. This wasn't something just for astronomers. It belonged to everyone."

Returning to Research

In 1998, Hammel became a Senior Research Scientist at the Space Science Institute in Boulder, Colorado, a position she holds to the present day. In addition, she is also the co-director of the Space Science Institute's Research Branch. Hammel works at her home office in Connecticut and travels extensively to conduct observational research, attend astronomy conferences, and speak on astronomy topics. She continues her research on the Ice Giants Neptune and Uranus.

"I am fascinated by the delicate balance of external radiation from the Sun and the internal heat from these planets.... We do not fully understand the physical processes involved in the balance, and yet it is the same balance that occurs in the Earth's atmosphere. In other words, by studying other planets, we learn about Earth, and knowledge of Earth is incredibly important to us as a species."

"What I like best about the planet Neptune is that every time you look at it, it's different, so Neptune can be *your* planet. The pictures that would be taken of Neptune would be yours. No one else would have seen the clouds that you see and they'll never be seen again probably. And so that means that the pictures of Neptune you take would be absolutely unique."

"With Uranus, now we're rewriting the textbooks on it. Our recent observations are so counter to what we thought.... We thought of Uranus's atmosphere as pretty much dead. And it's not," Hammel said. "Text-books describe Uranus as boring, but that's because the Voyager 2 probe flew by it during an uninteresting season.... We are now seeing the northern hemisphere for the first time, and the seasonal changes are fascinating to watch."

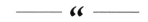

"So many people, especially women, think they're not qualified when it comes to new opportunities," Hammel observed. "You think there is someone who can do a job better, but usually there's not. Those guys who are acting like they are better qualified? They aren't any better qualified. They just think they are. Be willing to take a chance!"

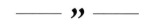

Planning for Deep Space Observation

In addition to conducting her own research, Hammel is a member of the team that is developing the James Webb Space Telescope. This telescope is expected to launch into space in 2018 and is intended to replace the Hubble Space Telescope. "I've been studying these planets for 20, 30 years now," Hammel said, "and we've really pushed the limits of what we can do from the ground and with Hubble." The James Webb Space Telescope will be capable of producing images of longer light wavelengths, allowing astronomers to look more closely at the oldest parts of the universe. Its mission will be to search for the first galaxies that were formed after the Big Bang, and determine how galaxies evolve over time.

"Each new discovery or observation or theory helps us better understand our universe. And that's important, but in some cases the new knowledge can be what we call incremental. It adds just a little bit of new understand-

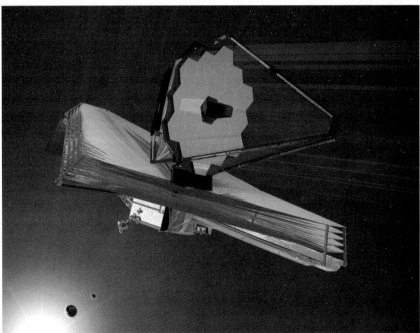

*Two images of the James Webb Space Telescope, now in construction:
a NASA engineer looks at the first six mirror segments, and an artist's vision
of how the telescope will look when complete.*

ing. For example, someone might have a model of the universe that says the universe is getting smaller with time. If your new data shows that the universe is getting smaller faster than the other person thought, this is important. But if your new data show that the universe is actually getting BIGGER with time, then that is IMPORTANT. See the difference? To do really IMPORTANT work usually requires either being exceedingly brilliant ... or being clever about which problem you choose and how you choose to solve it—like use a brand new instrument or work on a brand new field."

"If I see something that seems out of sync with what's already known, the first thing I do is try to find out what's wrong with the data. Once you've done that, and it still seems wrong, that's when things get interesting. It means you've found something new to understand. So you think about it and go for more data and come up with different models. All real science is like that."

Over the course of her long career, Hammel has established a reputation as one of the foremost planetary astronomers in the world. Planetary astronomers study the formation, development, and evolution of planets, including planetary atmosphere, weather, any satellites (such as moons), and any cosmic events that affect the planet. "You feel like you're exploring when you're doing planetary astronomy," she explained. "Maybe you're not physically walking on the surface of the planet, but you are exploring it for the first time. You're the pioneer."

"To be the best in a field always requires a lot of hard work. There are also still misperceptions that women don't do science, so one is always educating people about that. Girls especially seem to blame themselves if things go wrong (if they fail a test, or don't win a contest), and it takes a long time and plenty of self-coaching to get over that spurious limitation," Hammel said. "Don't turn down an opportunity because you are afraid. That's not a good reason to turn down something. So many people, especially women, think they're not qualified when it comes to new opportunities. You think there is someone who can do a job better, but usually there's not. Those guys who are acting like they are better qualified? They aren't any better qualified. They just think they are. Be willing to take a chance!"

MARRIAGE AND FAMILY

In 1996, Hammel married Tim Dalton, a chemical engineer. They live in Ridgefield, Connecticut, with their children: Beatrix, born in 1997, Tobias, born in 1999, and Lucas, born in 2001.

HONORS AND AWARDS

Harold C. Urey Prize (American Astronomical Society): 1996, for outstanding achievement by a young scientist

Spirit of American Women Award: 1996, for contributions to educational outreach

Named among the 50 Most Important Women Scientists (Discover): 2002

Carl Sagan Medal (American Astronomical Society's Division for Planetary Sciences): 2002, for outstanding communication of planetary science to the general public

FURTHER READING

Books

Beyond Jupiter: The Story of Planetary Astronomer Heidi Hammel, 2005

Periodicals

Astronomy, July 1997, p.50; Dec. 2010, p.50; Aug. 1, 2011
New York Times, Sep. 2, 2008; July 25, 2009, p.1
O, Dec. 2010
Sky & Telescope, Oct. 1995, p.6

Online Articles

www.fredbortz.com/HammelBio/AstroFAQ.htm
  (Dr. Fred's Place, "Heidi Hammel's Astronomy FAQ," Jan. 2006)
www.iwaswondering.org/heidi_homepage.html
  (IWasWondering.org, "Heidi Hammel," no date)
quest.nasa.gov/hst/PA-neptune.html
  (NASA, "Neptune," no date)
jwst.nasa.gov/meet-hammel.html
  (NASA James Webb Space Telescope, "Meet Heidi Hammel: Webb Telescope Interdisciplinary Scientist," no date)
www.thedailybeast.com/newsweek/2007/11/17/to-shoot-for-the-stars.html
  (Newsweek, "To Shoot For the Stars," Nov. 17, 2007)

ADDRESS

Heidi Hammel
Space Science Institute
4750 Walnut Street, Ste. 205
Boulder, CO 80301

WEB SITE

www.spacescience.org/about_ssi/staff/hammel.html

Steve Jobs 1955-2011
American Technology Pioneer and Business Leader
Co-Founder of Apple Inc. and Pixar

BIRTH

Steven Paul Jobs was born on February 24, 1955, in San Francisco, California. He was adopted by Paul Jobs, a machinist, and his wife Clara Jobs, who worked as an accountant. They raised him with a younger sister, Patty, adopted in 1957.

As an adult, Jobs traced the story of his birth parents. Joanne Schieble was a graduate student studying speech therapy at the University of Wisconsin. She fell in love with Abdulfattah

"John" Jandali, a teaching assistant in political science who was a Muslim from Syria. Schieble's father did not approve of the match, so when Schieble became pregnant she went to California to give the child up for adoption. Soon after, her father died and she and Jandali married. The marriage only lasted six years, and they had a daughter, Mona Simpson. Jobs met his birth mother and sister when he was in his 20s, but never contacted Jandali. His sister Mona remained one of his closest friends for the rest of his life.

YOUTH

Jobs was five when his family moved to the southern end of the San Francisco Bay area, home to so many technology companies that it would soon earn the name of "Silicon Valley." While it was clear young Steve was bright—his mother taught him to read before he started kindergarten—he did not always enjoy school. "When I got there I really just wanted to do two things," he noted. "I wanted to read books because I loved reading books and I wanted to go outside and chase butterflies." Jobs became a mischief maker, until his fourth grade teacher bribed him to complete his math workbook and get it right. "Before very long I had such a respect for her that it sort of re-ignited my desire to learn," he recalled. He skipped fifth grade but had trouble fitting in with his classmates. He was bullied so much in middle school he came home and announced he was never going back. Instead, the family moved to a new home in nearby Los Altos, which had better schools.

Jobs was only 10 or 11 when he was introduced to computers. His father took him to see the NASA Ames Research Center in nearby Sunnyvale, California, which had a computer. "I didn't see the computer, I saw a terminal and it was theoretically a computer on the other end of the wire," he recalled. "I fell in love with it."

Jobs's father supported his son in learning outside the classroom in other ways as well. Paul Jobs rebuilt and sold old cars as a side business and gave his son a special area in his garage workshop to work on his own projects. He introduced his son to the basics of electronics, and young Steve was soon fascinated. He was also encouraged by a neighbor, an engineer for electronics company Hewlett-Packard (HP). The neighbor introduced him to Heathkit-brand do-it-yourself electronics projects. Soon Jobs began assembling his own Heathkits. "It made you realize you could build and understand anything," he said. "Once you built a couple of radios, you'd see a TV in the catalogue and say, 'I can built that as well,' even if you didn't. I was very lucky, because when I was a kid both my dad and the Heathkits

IMPORTANT COMPUTER TERMS

Application Software: Software that is designed to help the user perform a specific task, such as word processing, designing graphics, or playing music, movies, or games. Often abbreviated to the term App.

Computer Processing Unit (CPU): The key component of all computers that carries out instructions of computer programs. Types of CPUs include circuit boards and microprocessors, also known as chips. A faster CPU makes for a more powerful computer.

Graphical User Interface (GUI): A method for a user to interact with computers by manipulating images (graphics) on the screen, usually with a mouse, rather than by typing text commands onto the screen with a keyboard.

Hardware: The physical "guts" of a computer, which may contain circuit boards, microchips, or similar CPU devices to process and store information.

Memory: Physical devices that can store instructions in a computer; these include magnetic tapes, magnetic disk drives, and optical disc drives, which use lasers. A larger memory makes for a more powerful computer.

Operating System (OS): A set of computer programs that manage a computer's hardware and provide a way for application software to communicate with the hardware. Common operating systems, besides Apple's iOS, include Microsoft Windows, UNIX, Linux, and Android (for mobile devices).

Software: A collection of computer programs that provide a computer with instructions of what tasks to perform and how to perform them. The term is often used to refer solely to application software.

System Software: Software, including operating systems, that manages computer hardware resources, telling them what to do and helping them communicate and run application software smoothly.

made me believe I could build anything." Jobs was 13 when, in the middle of building a device to measure electronic signals, he discovered a part missing. He looked up the home phone of William Hewlett, co-founder of HP, and called him directly. After talking to Hewlett for 20 minutes, Jobs secured the part as well as a summer internship on the HP assembly line.

EDUCATION

Jobs attended Homestead High School in Cupertino, California, where he was a member of the electronics club. After graduating in 1972, he enrolled at Reed College, a liberal arts college in Portland, Oregon. After one semester of required classes, he realized he was draining his parents' savings and not learning anything that interested him. Although he withdrew his enrollment, he became a "drop-in" rather than a dropout. He spent the next 18 months auditing classes, attending them without earning any credits toward a degree. He took only classes that interested him, including philosophy and calligraphy (the art of writing).

FIRST JOBS

Jobs came back to Silicon Valley in 1974 and found a job working for Atari, the video game company that had created the first hit video game, "Pong." After a few months he had saved enough money to finance a trip to India. He traveled throughout the country for seven months, exploring Eastern philosophy and seeking spiritual enlightenment. He returned to California in fall 1974 and returned to Atari.

By 1975 Jobs became involved with the Homebrew Computer Club, where he reconnected with Steve Wozniak, an older acquaintance he knew from his high school electronics club. Jobs and Wozniak had first collaborated in 1971 on a "blue box," an illegal device that used sound to fool telephones into giving the user free long-distance calls. They read about the machine, built one, and used it for pranks until Jobs suggested selling them. They sold almost 100 before being robbed of one at gunpoint. Although they quickly got out of the blue-box business, a few years later their common love of electronics would blossom into a partnership that transformed the computer industry.

CAREER HIGHLIGHTS

The Apple Computer Revolution

In the mid-1970s, when Jobs and Wozniak reconnected, computers were huge machines that could take up entire rooms; only businesses and universities could afford to buy and maintain them. Wozniak, however, had designed a simple standalone computer for hobbyists, consisting of a single circuit board as a central processing unit (CPU) that could be used at home with the owner's own video screen and keyboard. At first, Wozniak only intended the computer as a demonstration for the Homebrew Computer Club; it was Jobs who suggested they could sell the machine to computer

Jobs (right) with Apple co-founder Steve Wozniak from the company's early days.

enthusiasts. They founded Apple in 1976, dubbed the computer the Apple I, and Jobs soon got their first order—for 50 computers at $500 each—and financing to buy the parts. Wozniak, Jobs, and assorted friends and family members worked out of the Jobs family garage to complete the order. Jobs soon realized, however, that the do-it-yourself Apple I only appealed to hobbyists; their next product should be ready to run out of the box.

In 1977 the partners incorporated the company, rented offices, hired a president and a marketing firm, and chose the company's distinctive logo, an apple with a bite out of it. The Apple II launched that year and started the personal computer revolution: it included a built-in keyboard and speaker and even featured color graphics. While the insides were the product of Wozniak's electronics genius, the simple design and user-friendly case came from Jobs. When other computers still looked like scientific equipment, the Apple II was electronic equipment for the average consumer. The Apple II earned $2 million in its first year of sales, and by 1981 yearly sales were $600 million. When Apple Computer first began selling shares of the company to the public in December 1980, demand went through the roof. Four years after being founded for just over $5,000, Apple was worth $1.79 billion. At the age of 25, Jobs became a multi-millionaire. Rather than spend his new-found wealth, however, Jobs threw himself into working on two new products: the upgraded Apple III and the Lisa, a more powerful (and more expensive) personal computer.

A New Type of Computer: The Mac

Even as Apple engineers worked on these new—but not revolutionary—products, Jobs had another vision for the company. In 1979 he had visited the research center of Xerox, the copier and computer company, where he saw an experimental computer that used a mouse and a graphical user interface (GUI, pronounced "gooey") instead of typed commands. At this point, there were no computer icons (like the little pictures of a folder, a sheet of paper, and a trash can), no point and click, no drag and drop. Instead, computer users had to type in complicated sequences of commands and hold down multiple keys at a time, including the control, alt, tab, and function keys. It required far more expertise on the part of the user. For Jobs, seeing the new computer was a revelation. "It was one of those sort of apocalyptic moments," he recalled. "I remember within 10 minutes of seeing the graphical user interface stuff, just knowing that every computer would work this way someday. It was so obvious once you saw it. It didn't require tremendous intellect. It was so clear." Jobs went back to the Apple offices and immediately set his engineers to working on an operating system that would feature GUI and mouse.

——— **❝** ———

For Jobs, seeing an early computer with a graphical user interface and mouse was a revelation. "It was one of those sort of apocalyptic moments," he recalled. "I remember within 10 minutes of seeing the graphical user interface stuff, just knowing that every computer would work this way someday. It was so obvious once you saw it. It didn't require tremendous intellect. It was so clear."

——— **❞** ———

Two of the many Apple devices that revolutionized the industry: the Apple II (top), credited with launching the personal computer revolution; and the Macintosh (bottom), with a graphical user interface, mouse, and other features now common to all computers.

An impatient perfectionist, Jobs had a unique management style that developed from his passion for his work. He occasionally gave employees enthusiastic praise, but more often he offered only scornful criticisms or even insults. This was how Jobs tested his employees' enthusiasm for their ideas. One co-worker called his approach the "reality distortion field," because Jobs would refuse to accept scheduling or design limitations. By insisting that something could be done—often faster or better than before—Jobs goaded his employees into rising to the challenge. Some burned out and left the company, but others were inspired.

Under Jobs's direction, Apple engineers created the Macintosh, a simple, easy-to-use computer with a graphical user interface that changed the personal computing market. While Xerox first came up with the idea, Apple was the first to develop it for the personal computer, making the first commercially successful computer with a mouse and the features that are common on modern computers. As Jobs recalled, "The contributions we tried to make embodied values not only of technical excellence and innovation—which I think we did our share of—but innovation of a more humanistic kind."

The Macintosh was unveiled in 1984 with a groundbreaking Super Bowl commercial that portrayed Apple as breaking the conformist "Big Brother" mentality of their main competitor, computer giant IBM. The Mac's small memory meant sales were slow at first, but its graphical user interface, mouse control, and simplicity of use made it appeal to thousands of people who had never considered owning a personal computer before. The Mac changed people's perception of computers, convincing many that there was a market for personal computers for individuals, not just for businesses. The launch of the Mac was the second time that Jobs had changed the computer industry, according to *Fortune* writer Brent Schlender. "[Jobs] twice altered the direction of the computer industry. In 1977 the Apple II kicked off the PC era, and the graphical user interface launched by Macintosh in 1984 has been aped by every other computer since."

Apple's board of directors, however, was impatient. Sales of the error-prone Apple III and the expensive Lisa were dragging, and the Macintosh did not immediately take off. The board took away Jobs's power to make decisions for Apple products. In 1985, a frustrated Jobs was forced to resign from the company he had built.

New Directions: Pixar and the iMac

When Jobs left Apple, he saw a gap in the university market. Many science labs, for instance, needed individual computers more powerful than what the personal computer industry offered. He founded NeXT in 1985 to fill that gap by building a computer—both hardware and operating system—to meet that need. He sold all but one share of his Apple stock and got additional funding from financier (and future independent presidential candidate) Ross Perot. He built a state-of-the-art factory to produce the NeXT computer, a sleek black cube that debuted in 1988 with faster processing speeds, state-of-the-art graphics, and a new optical disc drive to provide computer memory. "I've always been attracted to the more revolutionary changes," Jobs noted. "I don't know why. Because they're harder. They're much more stressful emotionally. And you usually go through a period where everybody tells you that you've completely failed."

"I've always been attracted to the more revolutionary changes," Jobs noted. "I don't know why. Because they're harder. They're much more stressful emotionally. And you usually go through a period where everybody tells you that you've completely failed."

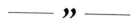

Jobs had always been interested in the intersection between computers and creative arts, once noting that "I actually think there's actually very little distinction between an artist and a scientist or engineer of the highest caliber." In 1986 he bought the graphics supercomputing division of Lucasfilm, the company founded by *Star Wars* director George Lucas, for $5 million. He immediately invested another $5 million in the company, which was incorporated as Pixar and initially developed high-end hardware, computers with powerful imaging capabilities that sold to medical facilities and intelligence agencies. Pixar's animation department, led by John Lasseter, initially existed to create short films that illustrated the capabilities of Pixar systems and software. But as sales of Pixar computers underperformed, the animation division developed a reputation for quality, with clever commercials and short films that won awards. After the Pixar short "Tin Toy" won the 1988 Academy Award for best animated short film, the company signed an agreement with Walt Disney Company, the pioneering animation studio, to produce the first feature-length computer-animated movie.

Disney liked Lasseter's story about two lost toys who try to find their way home, and production on Pixar's first full-length animated movie began in 1991. But the relationship between Disney and Pixar was rocky. Disney executives interfered with Pixar's ideas, so Jobs ran interference and kept

Woody, Buzz Lightyear, and the gang in Toy Story,
the first full-length Pixar feature film.

funding going when Disney threatened to pull out of the deal. During Pixar's first 10 years, Jobs spent another $50 million of his own money on the company, an investment that paid off in 1995 with the debut of *Toy Story*. Critics praised the film and audiences loved it; the film made $362 million worldwide and topped the U.S. charts for the year. Pixar also began selling shares of the company to the public in 1995. Their initial public offering (IPO) was the most successful of the year, with trading having to be delayed because of high demand. After the IPO, Jobs's shares—he owned 80 percent of the company—were worth $1.2 billion. Pixar's success resulted from more than Jobs's foresight, Pixar co-founder Edwin Catmull noted, "You need a lot more than vision—you need a stubbornness, tenacity, belief, and patience to stay the course. In Steve's case, he pushes right to the edge, to try to make the next big step forward. It's built into him."

Like Pixar's early imaging computers, the NeXT system did not sell as well as projected. (Nevertheless, it was used by programmer Tim Berners-Lee to create the first version of the World Wide Web in 1990.) Eventually Jobs decided the company should focus on producing operating systems instead of hardware. Its NeXTSTEP system was modestly successful, especially with computer programmers, and Jobs considered selling the company to focus on running Pixar. In the meantime, Apple Computer had suffered a downturn in sales and was behind schedule in developing an operating system for their next generation of computers. They bought NeXT in 1996 for $430 million and Jobs returned to Apple as an adviser. In September 1997 he became interim Chief Executive Officer (CEO) of Apple and faced the challenge of turning around a company whose share of the personal computing market had fallen to only four percent, from a high of 16 percent in the late 1980s.

Jobs set about changing the company's culture, which had chased profits with a confusing array of computers and devices. He decided Apple should focus on four core products: laptop and desktop computers for home and professional users. He found new board members who supported his goals, slashed development programs and personnel, and cut costs. He settled a patent lawsuit with Microsoft, whose GUI-based Windows operating system seemed to copy the Macintosh, and signed an agreement for Microsoft to make popular software programs available to Mac users. Jobs closely oversaw a new "Think Different" ad campaign for the company and drummed up excitement for Apple's new products. He also oversaw the beautiful new iMac, featuring a translucent blue case and a return to the revolutionary all-in-one design that had been popularized by the original Macintosh. When the iMac launched in 1998, it quickly became the best-selling computer in America. The portable iBook, with its bright colors and

Jobs with the iMac, known for its sleek all-in-one design.

distinctive clamshell shape, debuted in 1999 to similar excitement. In 2000, Jobs announced he would officially remain at Apple as its permanent CEO.

Reviving Apple with Music

The year 2001 was a turning point for Apple. Jobs was a firm believer in making products that integrated hardware, operating system, applications, and design to create a seamless experience for the user. In order to demonstrate these systems and provide customers with expert advice, he opened the first Apple store in 2001. While other computer manufacturers had failed with retail stores, Apple's emphasis on service and design—closely supervised by Jobs—made them a hit, grossing $1.4 billion in sales by 2004. Jobs also had a vision that in the future, home computers would serve as a hub, storing and organizing information for many portable digital machines. In fall 2001 Apple debuted the first of these portable devices, a music player dubbed the iPod. When integrated with Apple's free iTunes application, the iPod became an easy-to use music player that could play any of 1,000 songs with no more than three clicks. With the iPod, Apple transitioned from a computer company to a consumer electronics company. The iPod quickly became a hot seller, but Jobs had a further innovation planned for the music industry.

At that time, in the early 2000s, sharing music illegally on the internet had become widespread, and the music industry was suffering greatly from lost sales. Jobs proposed creating an online store that would sell single songs as well as entire albums, then he convinced nervous music companies to sign on by limiting the service to Apple users. The new iTunes Store was an instant success, selling one million songs in the first six days alone. More record companies signed on to the service, and it was opened to Windows users as well. For each 99-cent song sold on the iTunes store, Apple's share was only about a dime. But with one billion songs sold by 2006, those dimes added up. Internet advocates had predicted since the early 1990s that businesses could profit from these small "micropayments." But as Alan Deutschman argued in *Newsweek*, "It took Jobs and Apple to finally make it happen, and the execution was brilliant."

"[The iPod was not] the truly revolutionary advance that launched Apple on the path to dominance in the Internet era," Alan Deutschman wrote in Newsweek. *"The greatest breakthrough was really the iTunes store. ... The debut of iTunes marked the beginning of one of the most incredible winning streaks in the history of modern business, a breathtaking eight-year run."*

By 2008, Apple was the largest music retailer in the United States, with its music division providing almost 50 percent of company revenues. To date, iTunes has sold more than 16 billion song downloads. "[The iPod was not] the truly revolutionary advance that launched Apple on the path to dominance in the Internet era," Deutschman declared. "The greatest breakthrough was really the iTunes store, which went live in April 2003. The debut of iTunes marked the beginning of one of the most incredible winning streaks in the history of modern business, a breathtaking eight-year run."

At the same time, Jobs's other company, Pixar, was enjoying similar success. *Toy Story* was only the first in an unbroken string of critically acclaimed hit movies, including *Bug's Life, Toy Story 2, Monsters Inc., Finding Nemo, The Incredibles, Cars, Ratatouille,* and *Wall E.* In fact, *Finding Nemo* became the most successful animated movie to date when it debuted in 2003. Although Jobs had occasional conflicts with Disney management over their deal to market and distribute Pixar films, he listened when they offered to buy the company in 2006. The deal, in which Disney bought Pixar for $7.4 billion in stock, meant that Jobs gave up his title as Pixar

CEO. Instead, he joined Disney's board of directors as its largest single shareholder, with almost seven percent of the company's stock.

Meanwhile, Apple was making so much progress in developing electronic devices that in 2007 they dropped "computer" from the company title, becoming simply "Apple Inc." In 2005 the company had debuted the video iPod, making episodes of many popular television shows available on their iTunes Store. Two years later, with Jobs's usual flair for secrecy and style, Apple debuted the iPhone mobile phone. Unlike many personal digital devices of the time, the iPhone had no writing stylus; instead, it pioneered an unusual touch-screen interface that allowed customers to use two fingers to manipulate data and applications. Although it was the most expensive phone on the market, the iPhone outperformed projections, with 11.6 million sold by 2008. By the end of 2010, almost 90 million iPhones had been sold worldwide; sales almost doubled one year later, by the end of 2011, bolstered by the introduction of the iPhone 4S.

The next big Apple product was the iPad, a tablet computer featuring Apple's distinctive touch-screen interface and fun applications. The tablet computer had been around for almost 20 years, but the iPad was the first to energize the market. Again, Apple provided everything that its customers might need: it designed its own hardware, wrote its own software, sold products through its own stores, and delivered services through iTunes. The iPad sold one million units in its first month alone, with 15 million sold after nine months. In summer 2011, Apple introduced iCloud, an online storage service that integrated with all the company's various products.

Jobs was known for exerting complete control over every aspect of Apple's products. By creating one system designed by Apple, the company was able to integrate its hardware, software, design, content—even the retail store where the products were sold. This approach earned Jobs a reputation as a control freak. But others found value in his constant search for perfection, as Walter Isaacson argued in *Time* magazine, "There proved to be advantages to Jobs's approach. His insistence on end-to-end integration gave Apple, in the early 2000s, an advantage in developing a digital-hub strategy, which allowed you to link your desktop computer with a variety of portable devices and manage your digital content.... The result was that the iPod, like the iPhone and iPad that followed, was an elegant delight, in contrast to the kludgy rival products that did not offer such a seamless end-to-end experience.... In a world filled with junky devices, clunky software, inscrutable error messages, and annoying interfaces, Jobs' insistence on a simple, integrated approach led to astonishing products marked by delightful user experiences."

The iPhone (top), the iPod (left), and the iPad (bottom)—each device revolutionized its segment of the industry and changed people's lives.

A Lasting Legacy

Jobs was a workaholic accustomed to long hours. But he had also endured several health issues. He first developed kidney stones in 1997; a follow-up exam in 2004 showed he had developed pancreatic cancer. Although most pancreatic cancers are fatal within months, his cancer was a rare form that was treatable with surgery. Still, the experience made him conscious his time was limited. At a rare public speech at Stanford University's 2005 commencement, he told new graduates, "Remembering that you are going to die is the best way I know to avoid the trap of thinking you have something to lose. You are already naked. There is no reason not to follow your heart." He made plans for Apple to continue without him, hiring a chief operations officer to help manage the company and establishing "Apple University" to help employees understand the company's philosophy of management and product development. Still, in 2008 Jobs lost weight and looked ill, and speculation about his health led to a decline in stock prices. In early 2009, he announced he would take a medical leave from Apple to have a liver transplant. He was back at work at Apple offices within two months of his transplant.

By the beginning of 2011, Jobs announced that his cancer had returned and he began another medical leave. That August, he officially stepped down as CEO of Apple. "I've had a very lucky career, a very lucky life," he shared. "I've done all that I can do." Soon after, Apple became the world's most valuable company (in terms of the total value of all its stock).

Jobs died of complications from pancreatic cancer in Palo Alto, California, on October 5, 2011. News of his death led to spontaneous tributes from the public, as piles of flowers, notes, and apples were left at Apple stores around the world. Notable public figures paid tribute as well, including President Barack Obama. "Steve was among the greatest of American innovators—brave enough to think differently, bold enough to believe he could change the world, and talented enough to do it.... Steve was fond of saying that he lived every day like it was his last. Because he did, he transformed our lives, redefined entire industries, and achieved one of the rarest feats in human history: he changed the way each of us sees the world," Obama said. "The world has lost a visionary. And there may be no greater tribute to Steve's success than the fact that much of the world learned of his passing on a device he invented."

Many commentators remarked on the lasting influence Jobs had on technology and its role in our everyday lives. In naming Jobs CEO of the decade in 2009, *Fortune* senior editor Adam Lashinsky remarked that "in the past 10 years alone he has radically and lucratively reordered three

LeFT To RiGHT: LeoNARDO DaViNCi, ALeXANDeR GRAHAM BeLL, THOMAS EDiSON, THe New GUY

Jobs's death brought forth eulogies in many different forms, including this comment on his genius by cartoonist Steve Sack.

markets—music, movies, and mobile telephones—and his impact on his original industry, computing, has only grown." Business leader and New York City Mayor Michael Bloomberg observed, "Tonight, America lost a genius who will be remembered with Edison and Einstein, and whose ideas will shape the world for generations to come. Again and again over the last four decades, Steve Jobs saw the future and brought it to life long before most people could even see the horizon."

Some commentators marveled at what Jobs was able to achieve, as in these comments from Harry McCracken in *Time* magazine. "Steve Jobs … wasn't a computer scientist. He had no training as a hardware engineer or industrial designer," McCracken remarked. "The businesses Apple entered under his leadership—from personal computers to MP3 players to smart phones—all existed before the company got there. But with astonishing regularity, Jobs did something that few people accomplish even once: he reinvented entire industries. He did it with ones that were new, like PCs, and he did it with ones that were old, like music. And his pace only accelerated over the years. He was the most celebrated, successful business executive of his generation…. It's impossible to imagine what the past few

———— *"* ————

In a speech at Stanford University, Jobs once said that wonderful things happened in his life because he risked failure to do what he loved. "Your time is limited, so don't waste it living someone else's life.... Don't let the noise of others' opinions drown out your own inner voice. And most important, have the courage to follow your heart and intuition. They somehow already know what you truly want to become. Everything else is secondary."

———— *"* ————

decades of technology, business, and, yes, the liberal arts would have been like without him."

For technology writer Steven Levy, Jobs held a singular place in the history of invention. "If Jobs were not so talented, if he were not so visionary, if he were not so canny in determining where others had failed in producing great products and what was necessary to succeed, his pushiness and imperiousness would have made him a figure of mockery," Levy wrote in *Wired* magazine. "But Steve Jobs *was* that talented, visionary, and determined. He combined an innate understanding of technology with an almost supernatural sense of what customers would respond to. His conviction that design should be central to his products not only produced successes in the marketplace but elevated design in general, not just in consumer electronics but everything that aspires to the high end.... His accomplishments were unmatched. People who can claim credit for game-changing products—iconic inventions that become embedded in the culture and answers to Jeopardy questions decades later—are few and far between. But Jobs has had not one, not two, but *six* of these breakthroughs, any one of which would have made for a magnificent career. In order: the Apple II, the Macintosh, the movie studio Pixar, the iPod, the iPhone, and the iPad. (This doesn't even include the consistent, brilliant improvements to the Macintosh operating system, or the Apple retail store juggernaut.) Had he lived a natural lifespan, there would have almost certainly been more."

Speaking of his work, Jobs once commented, "My goal has always been not only to make great products, but to build great companies." Despite some failures, Jobs built not one but two great companies. By 2011, Pixar had grossed over $7.2 billion in worldwide box office sales, including *Toy Story 3*. the first animated film to make over a billion dollars worldwide. Apple was also left in strong shape, continuing to gain in stock value even

Apple CEO Tim Cooks speaks to employees at a celebration of Jobs's life.

during an economic downturn. Jobs called himself "a tool builder" who wanted to build tools "that I know in my gut and my heart will be valuable." He also noted that "technology is nothing. What's important is that you have a faith in people, that they're basically good and smart, and if you give them tools, they'll do wonderful things with them." Wonderful things happened in his life, he told his Stanford audience, because he risked failure to do what he loved. "Your time is limited, so don't waste it living someone else's life…. Don't let the noise of others' opinions drown out your own inner voice. And most important, have the courage to follow your heart and intuition. They somehow already know what you truly want to become. Everything else is secondary."

MARRIAGE AND FAMILY

Jobs was 23 when he had a daughter with Chrisann Brennan, his on-again, off-again girlfriend since high school. He initially denied paternity and had little involvement with the girl, named Lisa Brennan-Jobs. But they later reconciled and she spent her teen years living with him.

Jobs met Laurene Powell in 1990 when he was giving a lecture at Stanford University, where she was studying for her master's degree in business. They married on March 18, 1991, in Yosemite National Park. After their marriage Powell founded a natural foods company and started College

89

Track, a program matching mentors with disadvantaged students. She also kept busy raising their three children: son Reed Paul (born 1991) and daughters Erin Siena (born 1995) and Eve (born 1998).

HOBBIES AND OTHER INTERESTS

Growing up in the San Francisco area, Jobs was heavily influenced by the counterculture movement of the 1960s and early 1970s, which challenged authority and sought new means of self-expression. Jobs developed an early interest in Eastern philosophies, particularly Zen Buddhism, that lasted throughout his lifetime. He was also an early experimenter with both vegetarianism and veganism (not eating any animal products, including dairy and eggs) and tried various specialized diets throughout his life. Music, especially that of 1960s icons Bob Dylan and the Beatles, was another lifelong interest. While Jobs was not associated with any particular charities, he did involve Apple in several charitable initiatives, introducing a special red iPod as part of the (Product)RED campaign to benefit the Global Fund to Fight AIDS, Tuberculosis, and Malaria.

HONORS AND AWARDS

National Technology Medal (U.S. Department of Commerce): 1985, for "the creation of a cheap but powerful computer" (with Stephen Wozniak)
Jefferson Award for Public Service (American Institute for Public Service): 1987
Entrepreneur of the Decade (*Inc.*): 1989
Lifetime Achievement Award (Software Publishers Association): 1989
Vanguard Award (Producers Guild of America): 2002 (with Ed Catmull and John Lasseter)
Named #1 Most Powerful Person in Business (*Fortune*): 2007
CEO of the Decade (*Fortune*): 2009
Person of the Year (*Financial Times*): 2010
Inspire Award (AARP): 2012

FURTHER READING

Books

Isaacson, Walter. *Steve Jobs,* 2011

Periodicals

Current Biography Yearbook, 1983, 1998
Financial Times, Dec. 23, 2010, p.11
Fortune, Nov. 23, 2009, p.92

Newsweek, Sep. 5, 2011, p.30; Oct. 10, 2011, p.26
New York Times, Oct. 6, 2011, p.A1
New York Times Magazine, Jan. 12, 1997, p.6
Rolling Stone, June 16, 1994, p.73
Time, Jan. 3, 1983; Oct. 5, 2011
USA Today, Oct. 6, 2011, p.A1

Online Articles

www.businessweek.com
   (Business Week, "Technology Executives Comment on Steve Jobs's
   Death," Oct. 6, 2011)
www.computerhistory.org/highlights/stevejobs
   (Computer History Museum, "Steve Jobs: From Garage to World's Most
   Valuable Company," Dec. 8, 2011)
money.cnn.com
   (Money/CNN, "25 Most Powerful People in Business: #1. Steve Jobs,"
   July 11, 2007)
www.topics.nytimes.com
   (New York Times, "Steve Jobs," multiple articles, various dates)
www.nytimes.com
   (New York Times, "Steven P. Jobs, 1955-2011; Apple's Visionary Rede-
   fined Digital Age," Oct. 5, 2011)
americanhistory.si.edu/collections/comphist/sj1.html
   (Smithsonian Institution: Oral and Video Histories, "Steve Jobs Oral
   History," Computerworld Honors Program International Archives, Apr.
   20, 1995)
www.time.com/time/topics
   (Time, "Steve Jobs," multiple articles, various dates)
www.wired.com
   (Wired, "Steve Jobs, 1955-2011," "Steve Jobs' Greatest Achievements,"
   "Steve Jobs Through the Years," all Oct. 5, 2011)

WEB SITE

www.apple.com/stevejobs

Jennifer Lawrence 1990-
American Actress
Star of the Hit Movies *Winter's Bone, X-Men: First Class,* and *The Hunger Games*

BIRTH

Jennifer Shrader Lawrence was born on August 15, 1990, in Louisville, Kentucky. Her father, Gary, owned a concrete contracting business, and her mother, Karen, ran a children's camp. She has two older brothers named Ben and Blaine.

YOUTH

Lawrence grew up in the Indian Hills neighborhood of Louisville, Kentucky. Her brothers were very active in sports, and her parents encouraged her to participate as well. She tried field hockey and softball, but did not particularly enjoy playing those games. She became a cheerleader instead because she liked to do cartwheels and jump around.

As a young girl, Lawrence liked stories of all kinds. She liked watching movies and TV, reading, and listening to her parents and grandparents tell stories. She decided at a young age that she wanted to become a model or an actress. She acted in plays put on by her church, and also performed in productions of Shakespearean plays at the Walden Theatre in Louisville.

When she was 14 years old, Lawrence convinced her parents to take her to New York City during her spring break from school. The trip was more than a family vacation because she had also convinced her mother to meet with modeling and acting agencies. Her parents were reluctant to allow Lawrence to pursue her dream of acting. They thought her dream was unrealistic and only agreed to the trip because they thought it would help her "get the idea out of her system." "My parents were the exact opposite of stage parents," she recalled. "They did everything in their power to keep it from happening. But it was going to happen no matter what."

As it turned out, the trip did not prove to Lawrence that her acting ambition was foolish; instead, it put her on the path to becoming a professional actor. One day while they were walking around the city, Lawrence and her parents stopped to watch some street performers. They were approached by a man who said he was a photographer and that he was scouting for models for a TV commercial. "This guy was watching me, and he asked if he could take my picture," she explained. "We didn't know that that was creepy, at the time. So we're like, 'Sure.' So he took my mom's phone number, and all of a sudden all these agencies are calling. And that's when it all started."

The calls continued even after Lawrence and her parents returned home to Louisville. She begged her parents to let her return to New York and meet with some of the people who were calling. At first, her parents opposed the idea. They finally agreed after her brothers offered their opinions.

A scene from "The Bill Engvall Show," with Lawrence and Graham Patrick Martin.

Lawrence explained, "My two brothers said, 'Mom went to all our basketball and football games and travelled all around the country for us. She would do it for us if it were sports. This is Jen's sport.'"

That summer, Lawrence's parents allowed her to return to New York for two months. They rented an apartment in the city and had various family members take turns staying there with her, taking her to auditions and meetings. Though her parents expected it to be a temporary arrangement, Lawrence knew it was the beginning of her career. "I just started getting an overwhelming feeling of being exactly where I needed to be exactly when I had to be there. Every time I would leave an agency and stop reading a script, I just wanted to keep going and going."

EDUCATION

Lawrence graduated from Kammerer Middle School in Louisville. She wanted to continue to focus on acting, so she persuaded her parents to allow her to study independently instead of enrolling in high school. She earned a GED in just two years, studying while she worked and went to auditions in New York City and Los Angeles. (A GED, or General Equivalency Diploma, is a certification that a person has the academic skills and knowledge that are typically attained through a high school education.) Earning a GED was one of the conditions required by her parents. They insisted that Lawrence must complete her high school education if she wanted to continue acting.

CAREER HIGHLIGHTS

Lawrence started out as an actor with appearances in television commercials. She also had small guest spots on popular TV shows like "Monk," "Cold Case," and "Medium." Her first larger role was in the 2006 television movie *Company Town*, about a group of government agents who all live in the same neighborhood in Washington, DC. *Company Town* was created as the pilot for a TV series, though the series was never produced. In 2007, Lawrence appeared in the pilot episode for the TV series "Not Another High School Show," a parody of TV shows about the lives of high school students.

Lawrence landed her first role on a TV series in 2007, on the situation comedy "The Bill Engvall Show." Set in a suburb of Denver, Colorado, this family comedy centered on the life of Bill Pearson, played by comedian Bill Engvall. Each episode of the show focused on the challenges Pearson faces as a husband and parent. Lawrence played Pearson's teenaged daughter Lauren, a typical high school student making her way through dating, homework, and life with two brothers. "The Bill Engvall Show" aired for three seasons, from 2007-2009. In 2009, Lawrence won a Young Artist Award for Outstanding Young Performers in a TV Series, which she shared with her co-stars.

Becoming a Movie Actor

Lawrence began appearing in movies while she was still acting on "The Bill Engvall Show." She worked on movies during her breaks from filming episodes of the show and had roles in three movies that were released in 2008. Lawrence had a small part in *Garden Party*, the tragic story of a group of confused teens who are on their own in Los Angeles as they chase their dreams. Her first starring role was in the dark, gritty drama *The Poker House*. In this movie, Lawrence played Agnes, a teenager struggling to raise her younger sisters in the chaotic home of their mother, a prostitute who also runs a gambling operation in their house. In the dark and intense drama *The Burning Plain*, she played Mariana, a troubled young woman trying to overcome her mother's death. In 2009, Lawrence appeared in the movie *Devil You Know*, a tense drama about a former movie star who is blackmailed when she tries to restart her career.

These movies were independent films that were not widely released in theaters, though each role helped Lawrence gain acting experience and

A scene from Winter's Bone.

exposure that would benefit her career. She quickly gained a reputation for playing challenging roles with a maturity and acting ability beyond her years. "When you first start acting, you can't pick and choose," she observed. "Those were the roles I was booking. It was me, the girl from Kentucky with the wonderful family. Everyone was seeing this ability to go to this dark place that I didn't know that I had. I auditioned for every comedy, everything under the sun. I'm not going to pretend that I've been smart to pick these things. I've auditioned for all of those, but the comedies and the lovey-dovey movies didn't pick me."

Winter's Bone

Lawrence's early roles portraying difficult characters in dark dramatic stories led to her breakout role as the star of *Winter's Bone*, released in 2010. This critically acclaimed independent film was based on the 2006 novel by Daniel Woodrell. Lawrence played the role of Ree Dolly, a 17-year-old girl living in the rural Ozark Mountains of southern Missouri. With her drug-dealing addict father in prison, Ree desperately struggles to care for her ailing mother and two younger siblings. After her father goes missing, Ree must find him before the court seizes the family's home and land, which he put up for his bail bond. The harsh realities of Ree's difficult life unfold as she tries to uncover the details of her father's fate.

The role of Ree gave Lawrence an opportunity to showcase her acting ability. Even though *Winter's Bone* was not widely seen by general moviegoers, Lawrence's performance captivated film critics. As *Variety* movie reviewer Justin Chang wrote, "The film's atmosphere of suspicion, foreboding, and everyday misery would be too much to bear if not for the rich emotional anchor supplied by Lawrence. Emphasizing Ree's patience, maturity, and love for her siblings as much as her tenacity and courage, Lawrence delivers a striking portrait of someone who, though looked down upon by many for her youth and gender, alone seems to possess the guts and smarts necessary to survive and possibly even escape her surroundings." Writing in *The New Yorker*, David Denby praised Lawrence's acting: "Her Ree is the head of a household, a womanly girl with no time for her own pleasure, and Lawrence establishes the character's authority right away, with a level stare and an unhurried voice that suggest heavy lifting from an early age. The movie would be unimaginable with anyone less charismatic playing Ree."

For her performance in *Winter's Bone,* Lawrence won a New Hollywood Award in 2010. She was nominated for a host of awards in 2011, including an Academy Award for Best Performance by an Actress in a Leading Role, a Golden Globe Award for Best Performance by an Actress in a Motion Picture—Drama, and a Screen Actors Guild Award, for Outstanding Performance by a Female Actor in a Leading Role. She was also nominated for two Broadcast Film Critics Association Critics Choice Awards, for Best Actress and Best Young Actor/Actress, an Independent Spirit Award, for Best Female Lead, and a Young Artist Award, for Best Performance in a Feature Film—Leading Young Actress. Lawrence's portrayal of Ree Dolly earned her a 2011 National Board of Review Award, for Breakthrough Performance.

Lawrence followed the success of *Winter's Bone* with a part in the 2011 romantic drama *Like Crazy.* This movie tells the story of two university students, one American and one British, who must decide if their love is worth fighting for through complicated government rules and immigration laws. She also appeared in the 2011 dark comedy *The Beaver,* about a psychologically troubled man who only communicates through the use of a hand puppet shaped like a beaver.

X-Men: First Class

Lawrence's next big role was in the 2011 action movie *X-Men: First Class.* This installment of the popular movie series based on the *X-Men* comic books chronicles the origins of the first X-Men superheroes. Lawrence plays the young Raven Darkholme, who will become the mutant superhero known as Mystique. (The role of Mystique as an adult is played in previous X-Men movies by Rebecca Romijn.) Young Raven is insecure

Castmates from X-Men: First Class. *From left: Michael Fassbender as Erik (Magneto), Caleb Landry Jones as Banshee, James McAvoy as Charles (Professor Xavier), Rose Byrne as Moira, Jennifer Lawrence as Raven (later Mystique), and Lucas Till as Havok.*

about her natural appearance—she has bright yellow eyes and a blue body covered in scales. She can change her appearance to duplicate any human, so she chooses to appear most of the time as a "normal" girl. But if she is to fully embrace her superpowers, Raven must learn to fully accept her true self. Raven's self-acceptance is encouraged by her friendship with young Xavier and aided by the discovery of other young mutants.

As the young mutants find each other and come together under the direction of Xavier, they each discover that they are not the only ones with special powers. Learning that they are not alone in the world as freaks and outsiders, the young mutants decide to become the X-Men and use their powers to benefit all mankind. Their first challenge is to stop the beginning of World War III, a crisis that ultimately forces former friends and allies Xavier and Magneto to become sworn enemies. The other mutants choose sides, and the conflict between the X-Men and Magneto's Brotherhood begins.

To become the blue-skinned Raven/Mystique, Lawrence had to undergo an elaborate and time-consuming makeup process. Every day, seven makeup artists painted her body with six layers of blue paint, followed by five layers of spackling, and finished with hundreds of scales that had to be glued on one by one. This process took eight to ten hours each day. For her performance, Lawrence was nominated for two 2011 Teen Choice Awards, for Choice Movie Breakout: Female, and Choice Movie Chemistry, which she shared with her co-stars. Lawrence was also nominated for a 2012 People's Choice Award for Favorite Movie Superhero.

The Hunger Games

After *X-Men: First Class,* Lawrence's next major project was the starring role in the highly anticipated 2012 movie *The Hunger Games.* The movie is based on the first book in the wildly popular three-book series by Suzanne Collins: *The Hunger Games, Catching Fire,* and *Mockingjay. The Hunger Games* tells the story of fierce and determined Katniss Everdeen. Katniss is a 16-year-old girl living in the brutal world of Panem, a nation that evolved from the remains of North America after a terrible calamity. Most of the citizens of Panem's 12 districts are forced to work to support the wealthy, tyrannical rulers of the Capitol. Many years before Katniss was born, the people in the districts went to war against the Capitol and suffered a terrible defeat. As part of their surrender, each district was forced to agree to send one boy and one girl to participate in "The Hunger Games," an annual televised competition. The 24 competitors, known as "tributes," are selected by lottery. They are taken to the Capitol and locked in an arena where they must fight one another to the death, until only one is left alive. The winner is awarded riches and freedom. An expert hunter and archer, Katniss becomes a tribute for her district. *The Hunger Games* tells the story of her experiences in the gruesome competition.

> *"The cool thing about Katniss is that every fan has such a personal relationship with her, and they understand and know her in a singular way," Lawrence said. "I'm a massive fan too, so I get it." Even Suzanne Collins was impressed with Lawrence: "I never thought we'd find somebody this perfect for the role."*

The casting of Lawrence as Katniss initially set off tremendous controversy among fans of the books. Many were concerned that Lawrence was completely wrong for the role, because she is too pretty, too old, too tall, too athletic, too pale, and too blonde. As a fan of *The Hunger Games* series herself, Lawrence shared some of the same concerns. "The cool thing about Katniss is that every fan has such a personal relationship with her, and they understand and know her in a singular way. I'm a massive fan too, so I get it." Everyone's fears were eased when Lawrence was approved by Collins, who said, "I never thought we'd find somebody this perfect for the role."

Lawrence was pleased to have the support of author Suzanne Collins and film director Gary Ross. "[Katniss is] incredibly powerful, brave, and tough

Lawrence as Katniss in a scene from The Hunger Games.

and yet she has a tenderness and complexity," Lawrence said. "It was very humbling hearing that Suzanne and Gary feel that I embody those traits." Lawrence threw herself into preparing for the role of Katniss. She learned archery from a former Olympic champion and followed an intense physical training program to prepare for the action scenes and stunts. Already a fan of the books, Lawrence also worked hard on developing her approach to the character that would be portrayed on screen. "I'm really picky about the projects I do. I don't really like stories that don't take you anywhere. That's what a film is, it's a journey. I ask myself, 'What is this character like at the beginning and what must I do to get her to the end?'"

The Hunger Games movie was developed under strict secrecy requirements, and few details were revealed about the movie in advance of its release. Collins explained that the story of the movie does not follow exactly along with the story presented in the book. "When you're adapting a novel into a two-hour movie you can't take everything with you," Collins acknowledged. "The story has to be condensed to fit the new form. Then there's the question of how best to take a book told in the first person and present tense and transform it into a satisfying dramatic experience. In the novel, you never leave Katniss for a second and are privy to all of her thoughts, so you need a way to dramatize her inner world and make it possible for other characters to exist outside of her company.... A lot of things are acceptable on a page that wouldn't be on a screen."

Katniss (Lawrence) being escorted by Capitol guards,
before the start of the Hunger Games.

Response to the Movie

The Hunger Games movie was released in March 2012, with Lawrence in the role of Katniss joined by Liam Hemsworth as Gale, Josh Hutcherson as Peeta, Woody Harrelson as Haymitch Abernathy, Elizabeth Banks as Effie, Lenny Kravitz as Cinna, and Donald Sutherland as President Snow. Immediate response from the public was overwhelming, and ticket sales soared as the book's many fans came to see how the movie lived up to their expectations. Critical response was a bit mixed. Many critics noted that the movie showed enough of the characters and the action of the books to satisfy, if not enthrall, the book's fans. Several argued that the filmmakers' desire to secure a PG-13 rating meant that some of the more violent scenes in the book had been toned down—yet they also noted that many horrific and gruesome elements still remained. Several reviewers suggested that the movie failed to explain the reasons behind the characters' actions and also failed to explore the book's larger themes. "The movie shows how," Lisa Schwarzbaum wrote in *Entertainment Weekly*, "but the book shows why."

Many critics offered both criticism and praise of the movie, with special admiration for Lawrence's performance. "This *Hunger Games* is a muscular, honorable, unflinching translation of Collins's vision," Schwarzbaum also wrote. "It's brutal where it needs to be, particularly when children fight and bleed. It conveys both the miseries of the oppressed, represented by the poorly fed and clothed citizens of Panem's 12 suffering districts, and the rotted values of the oppressors, evident in the gaudy decadence of those who live in the Capitol. Best of all, the movie effectively showcases the allure of the story's remarkable, kick-ass 16-year-old heroine, Katniss Everdeen. ... [Jennifer Lawrence] is, in her gravity, her intensity, and her own unmannered beauty, about as impressive a Hollywood incarnation of Katniss as one could ever imagine."

"When you're talking about *The Hunger Games*, it all comes down to Katniss," Kenneth Turan wrote in the *Los Angeles Times*. "Making a successful *Hunger Games* movie out of Suzanne Collins's novel required casting the best possible performer as Katniss, and in Jennifer Lawrence director Gary Ross and company have hit the bull's-eye, so to speak. An actress who specializes in combining formidable strength of will with convincing vulnerability, Lawrence is the key factor in making *Hunger Games* an involving popular entertainment with strong narrative drive that holds our attention by sticking as close to the book's outline as it can manage. ... Lawrence's ability to involve us in [Katniss's] struggle is a key to the effectiveness of *Hunger Games*."

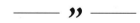

"[Jennifer Lawrence] is, in her gravity, her intensity, and her own unmannered beauty, about as impressive a Hollywood incarnation of Katniss as one could ever imagine." — Lisa Schwarzbaum, **Entertainment Weekly**

"Relax, you legions of Hunger Gamers. We have a winner. Hollywood didn't screw up the film version of Suzanne Collins's young-adult bestseller," Peter Travers wrote in *Rolling Stone*. "The screen *Hunger Games* radiates a hot, jumpy energy that's irresistible. It has epic spectacle, yearning romance, suspense that won't quit, and a shining star in Jennifer Lawrence, who gives us a female warrior worth cheering. As 16-year-old Katniss Everdeen ... Lawrence reveals a physical and emotional grace that's astonishing. Give her the deed, because she owns this movie. ... My advice is to keep your eyes on Lawrence, who turns the movie into a victory by presenting a heroine propelled by principle instead of hooking up with the cutest boy. That's what makes Katniss revolutionary. May the odds be ever in her favor."

Other Projects

Lawrence's future plans include continuing to act and someday becoming a director. She has a starring role in the 2012 horror movie *The House at the End of the Street,* about a mother and daughter who move into a house near the one where a young girl murdered her parents—and soon learn there is more to that story than anyone knew. She also stars in the 2012 comedy *The Silver Linings Playbook,* about a man who tries to rebuild his life after four years in a mental hospital. Lawrence will also appear in the future *Hunger Games* movies.

Lawrence is philosophical in reflecting on the successes that she has achieved thus far in her career. She believes that her success as an actor is at least partially out of her hands. "I'd love to take credit for it. But I was just like every actress in L.A. that auditions for everything, and those were the roles that picked me. I could try to plan everything—and I have, of course, because I'm controlling—but I've watched my career take shape, and I love what it's done. I never could have designed that in a million years."

"You work so hard for something. Mostly, I'm just really happy that I've been able to do what I love. I know that sounds kind of simple, but I've found something I really love doing and I can do it every day of my life. That's what I'm most excited about. The recognition and the parties are great—it's an honor—but I'm mostly just excited to be here working."

HOME AND FAMILY

When she is not filming a movie, Lawrence divides her time between homes in New York City and Santa Monica, California. She lives with her dog, a Yorkshire terrier named Alden.

SELECTED CREDITS

"The Bill Engvall Show," 2007-2009 (TV series)
Winter's Bone, 2010
The Beaver, 2011
Like Crazy, 2011
X-Men: First Class, 2011
The Hunger Games, 2012

HONORS AND AWARDS

Young Artist Award: 2009, Outstanding Young Performers in a TV Series, for "The Bill Engvall Show" (shared with co-stars)
National Board of Review Award: 2010, Breakthrough Performance, for *Winter's Bone*
New Hollywood Award: 2010, for *Winter's Bone*

FURTHER READING

Periodicals

Entertainment Weekly, Mar. 27, 2011, p.34; Aug. 5, 2011, p.44
Flare, June 2011, p.126
Interview, Nov. 2010, p.84
People, June 6, 2011, p.38
Teen Vogue, May 2011
USA Today, June 9, 2010, p.D1
Wall Street Journal, May 27, 2011, p.D5

Online Articles

www.theglobeandmail.com
  (Globe and Mail, "Thanks for Raising Me, But I'm Going to Take it from
  Here,"June 11, 2010)
www.louisville.com
  (Louisville, "Too Young for Methods: Louisville's Academy Award-Nom-
  inated Actress Jennifer Lawrence,"Feb. 9, 2011)
www.manhattanmoviemag.com
  (Manhattan Movie Magazine, "Jennifer Lawrence Is the Breakout Star of
  Winter's Bone,"June 12, 2010)
louisville.metromix.com
  (Metromix Louisville, "Jennifer Lawrence: Bigger Things,"Oct. 14, 2009)

ADDRESS

Jennifer Lawrence
PO Box 6509
Louisville, KY 40206

WEB SITE

jenniferslawrence.com

Manny Pacquiao 1978-
Filipino Boxer and Political Leader
World Boxing Titleholder in Eight Different Weight
Classes
Member of the Filipino House of Representatives

BIRTH

Emmanuel "Manny" Dapidran Pacquiao (PAK-ee-ow) was
born on December 17, 1978, in the Republic of the Philippines. He was born in the town of Kibawe, which is located in
the province of Bukidnon on the island of Mindanao, one of
the largest islands in the Philippines. Altogether, the Philip-

pines consist of more than 7,000 islands clustered in the western Pacific Ocean off the coast of southwest Asia.

Manny's mother is Dionisia Dapidran, who supported her four children by farming, cleaning houses, doing other people's laundry, and selling peanuts and other foods as a street vendor. His father is Rosalio Pacquiao, who worked as a farm hand and manual laborer. He abandoned his wife and children when Manny was a small child.

YOUTH

Although Pacquiao was born in Kibawe, at age two his mother moved the family to an isolated mountain settlement called Tango. The village was located in a densely forested section of the Philippine province of Sarangani. "The jungle was the greenest of green and was populated with every multicolored bird you can imagine," he recalled in his memoir, *Pac-Man*. "I can still clearly recall how very difficult it was for my family to trudge up and down the rocky, dirt-covered road several times a week to get everything we needed to survive. While helping my mother, sister, and brothers lug the heavy buckets of water and the old burlap bags of rice and flour on the steep road, I loved to hear the songs these birds sang."

The Pacquiao family lived in a one-room thatch-covered hut. Each day Manny and his mother and siblings left their home in search of food and fresh water. He remembered that when he and his brothers and sisters were not at school or carrying supplies from town, "we were cooking, tending my mother's small garden, and doing any number of other chores assigned to us." Years later, he wrote that "I was about 10 years old before I fully appreciated ... how close we were to perishing in the harsh jungle environment."

The family's difficult everyday existence left Pacquiao with little time to play or engage in other ordinary childhood pursuits. "I had no concept of toys, television, household appliances, or even a bed that most of us today

> *Pacquiao's family was very poor, which left him with little time to play or engage in other ordinary childhood pursuits. "I had no concept of toys, television, household appliances, or even a bed that most of us today would consider necessities," he said. "My toys were rocks and trees, and my bed was a blanket on a dirt floor."*

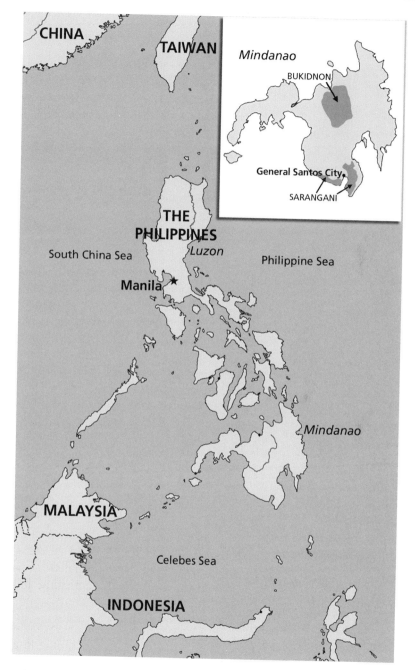

A map of the Philippines, showing portions of China, Taiwan, Malaysia, and Indonesia. The inset map shows the island of Mindanao; the provinces of Bukidnon and Sarangani; and General Santos City.

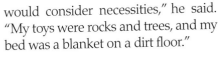

"I could go long stretches without eating, but it always pained me to see my mother, two brothers, and my sister with that vacant and hopeless look of hunger in their eyes," Pacquiao wrote.

would consider necessities," he said. "My toys were rocks and trees, and my bed was a blanket on a dirt floor."

When Pacquiao was 10 years old his mother decided that life on the mountain was just too hard on her children. She packed the family possessions into a few burlap bags and moved her children to General Santos City, a big port city in the south of Mindanao. They settled into one of the city's vast slum neighborhoods, and she found work as a housecleaner and laundress.

All the children pitched in as well, working at whatever odd jobs they could find to supplement their mother's hard-earned but meager earnings. Manny's main contribution came as a street vendor. He became skilled at buying donuts, peanuts, bread, and other food items from street sellers and small stores—then turning around and selling these items to customers at a small profit. "By the time I was 13, I was a one-man traveling grocery store,"Pacquiao wrote. "Imagine this small, wiry, hungry boy carrying a box of warm donuts down those dusty, hot streets. The smell was irresistible, and I could easily have chosen to eat all five donuts.... But I knew if I ate them, I would be hungrier later, and so would my family."

Years later, Pacquiao described his daily refusal to give in to temptation and eat those donuts as a defining moment in his youth. "The discipline and willpower those donuts forced me to develop have served me well all my life," he explained. "Patience is a virtue, especially when you are in survival mode."

Starting to Box

Pacquiao's childhood and early adolescence were marked by a lot of scrapes with other kids in his rough and sometimes-violent neighborhood. He did not really think about pursuing a boxing career, though, until age 12, when he saw a televised heavyweight title fight between Mike Tyson and James "Buster" Douglas. Everyone thought Tyson would crush the lightly regarded Douglas, but instead the underdog shocked the world by knocking out Tyson in the 10th round.

The bout made a big impression on Pacquiao. "It was then that I learned that even champions could never count on their wins, that they have to earn them every single time," he wrote. "To this day, I still watch replays of that fight because it still amazes me."

Within a matter of weeks Pacquiao became a regular at the neighborhood boxing ring, which was located in a rundown park down the street. "I fought at this park for two years until I had beaten everyone, including the much bigger and heavier kids," he remembered. "As I trained and gained muscle, there was no one I could not beat."

On His Own in Manila

When Pacquiao was 14 years old he made a momentous choice. He decided to stow away on a ship that was bound for the national capital of Manila, about 500 miles away from General Santos City. Years later, he explained in his memoir that he slipped away to Manila because it would give his mother one less mouth to feed. "I could go long stretches without eating, but it always pained me to see my mother, two brothers, and my sister with that vacant and hopeless look of hunger in their eyes," he wrote.

Pacquiao struggled to survive on the streets of Manila. Some days he would go without food, and he spent many nights sleeping in alleyways or under bridges. As time passed, though, he managed to find work as a gardener, construction worker, restaurant dishwasher, and welder. Whenever he accumulated a little extra money he sent it back to his family.

EDUCATION

Pacquiao's family was so poor that he was forced to drop out of school at age 12. By leaving school he could devote more time to earning money for food and other basic necessities. The decision, though, brought a lot of feelings of regret. He liked his classes, and he enjoyed challenging himself with schoolwork. "[Pacquiao] never cheated during a quiz—he wouldn't try to look sideways, this way or that," recalled one of his elementary school teachers.

Long after Pacquiao became a successful and wealthy boxer, his skimpy educational background continued to bother him. He became so determined to address the issue that he began studying for a General Equivalency Diploma (GED) in the United States. In 2007 he passed his GED test, which is recognized as the equivalent of a regular high school diploma.

CAREER HIGHLIGHTS

Pacquiao continued his boxing training after his arrival in Manila. For a time he even slept at the gym where he trained. At age 16 he decided that he was ready to "turn pro"—become a paid professional boxer.

WEIGHT CLASSIFICATIONS

Professional boxers compete against one another in a series of categories based on weight classifications. The list below shows the maximum weight for each category.

light flyweight	108 pounds
flyweight	112 pounds
super flyweight	115 pounds
bantamweight	118 pounds
super bantamweight	122 pounds
featherweight	126 pounds
super featherweight	130 pounds
lightweight	135 pounds
super lightweight/ junior welterweight	140 pounds
welterweight	147 pounds
super welterweight	154 pounds
middleweight	160 pounds
super middleweight	168 pounds
light heavyweight	175 pounds
cruiserweight	200 pounds
heavyweight	unlimited

Pacquiao's first professional boxing match, on January 22, 1995, was televised on a popular Filipino boxing program called "Blow by Blow," which broadcast several bouts every week. He made his debut as a light flyweight, which is the lightest weight classification in boxing. The left-handed Pacquiao won his first match in a four-round decision. He only made two dollars for the fight—and for each of his next several appearances on "Blow by Blow"—but he still managed to send most of his earnings to his mother to help her provide for his siblings.

Earning His First Two Boxing Titles

Pacquiao won his first 11 bouts. Each time he stepped into the ring, he displayed sharp fighting skills and a sort of boyish enthusiasm that made him a favorite among Filipino boxing fans. Pacquiao lost his 12th match to Rustico Torrecampo in a third-round knockout, but the feisty boxer quickly recovered. He won his next 12 fights—10 by knockout (KO) or technical knockout (TKO), which is when the referee stops the bout because he feels one boxer is too badly injured to keep competing.

Pacquiao's winning streak earned him a title fight against Thailand's Catchai Sasakul, the World Boxing Council (WBC) flyweight champion. Professional boxing includes several different organizations that crown their own champions in the various weight classes. Boxers can hold more than one organizational title at a time, but it is not unusual for a single weight class to have multiple "champions" recognized by different organizations. On December 4, 1998, Pacquiao knocked out Sasakul in the eighth round to earn his first major boxing title.

Pacquiao held the title for nine months, successfully defending his crown in two bouts. But on September 17, 1999, he was knocked out in the third round of a fight against Thailand's Medgoen Singsurat. The loss was a big disappointment to Pacquiao—or Pac-Man, as he was coming to be known by boxing fans.

After losing to Singsurat, Pacquiao skipped the super flyweight and bantamweight divisions and moved all the way up to super bantamweight. Fighting at 122 pounds, Pacquiao won five bouts in a row. These dominating performances gave him an opportunity to win his second major title. In June 2001 organizers of a Las Vegas fight approached Pacquiao. The organizers were planning a fight featuring International Boxing Federation (IBF) super bantamweight champion Lehlo Ledwaba, and they asked Pacquiao if he would be willing to be a last-minute replacement for the scheduled challenger. Delighted at the chance to earn his second major title, Pacquiao quickly agreed, even though he had been told that Ledwaba "was so ferocious that his own managers were sometimes scared to deal with him."

Pacquiao immediately flew to Los Angeles for intensive pre-fight training. Within a day or two of his arrival he began training with Freddie Roach, who owned a fight gym in town. The two men connected immediately, and Roach has remained the boxer's chief trainer since that day.

On June 23, 2001—only two weeks after being offered the fight—Pacquiao scored a sixth-round knockout of Ledwaba. "After the first round, I don't think he knew what hit him," Pacquiao later wrote in his memoir. "I was in a zone and I would not be denied this victory. Part of my iron will was that I was prepared mentally for anything. My vow was just as strong. This was going to be my night."

Building a Better Boxer

Pacquiao defended his IBF super bantamweight title four times before moving up to the 126-pound featherweight division. In his first fight in

113

Pacquiao raises his arm in victory after defeating Lehlohonolo Ledwaba, June 2001.

that class, he knocked out Mexico's Marco Antonio Barrera on November 15, 2003, to become *The Ring* magazine's world featherweight champion.

Pacquiao's next major fight came in May 9, 2004, when he faced off against Juan Manuel Márquez, who held both the WBA (World Boxing Association) and IBF world featherweight titles at the time. Pacquiao managed to knock the champion to the canvas three times early in the fight, but Márquez came back strong in the later rounds. The fight ended up a draw. One judge scored the champ as the winner, another favored Pacquiao, and the third scored it a tie. The draw became a controversial decision that angered both boxers, each of whom believed that he deserved the win.

In early 2005 Pacquiao moved up yet another weight class in a bid to unseat super featherweight world champion Erik Morales. This March 19 match ended in defeat for Pacquiao, who lost a unanimous decision from the judges. The setback, though, just motivated Pacquiao and Roach to work even harder at developing the boxer's skills. Week after week, they labored to improve the boxer's already amazing hand speed, endurance, and boxing technique. During this time the two men paid particular attention to improving the punching power in Pacquiao's right hand.

> ———— " ————
>
> *"Pac-Man's style still features feverish punches and constant motion," Pablo S. Torre observed in* Sports Illustrated. *"The southpaw lets out a yell with every punch (Boom!) and combination (Boomboomboom!). If he takes a hard shot, he'll bang his gloves together, stick his arms into the air, and grin broadly."*
>
> ———— " ————

On September 10, 2005, Pacquiao knocked out Héctor Velázques in the sixth round to capture the WBC super featherweight crown. This marked the fourth weight class in which Pac-Man had risen to the top of his profession. Four months later, he stepped into the ring against Morales again. By this time Morales had lost his title to another boxer, but he remained a formidable opponent. Determined to avenge his 2005 loss to Morales, Pacquiao applied relentless pressure from the opening bell. He finally knocked Morales out in the 10th round—the first time that Morales had been KO'd in his boxing career.

Pacquiao successfully defended his super featherweight title four more times in 2006-2007, drawing big crowds each time. These triumphs included a unanimous decision over former bantamweight champ Oscar Larios (on July 2, 2006, in Quezon City, Philippines), another knockout of Morales (on November 18, 2006, in Las Vegas), and an easy unanimous decision in a rematch with Barrera (on October 6, 2007, in Las Vegas). These impressive performances resulted in a cascade of special honors from boxing organizations. In addition, growing numbers of boxing experts declared that the hard-hitting Filipino was the best "pound-for-pound" fighter in the world.

Claiming New Titles

On March 15, 2008, Pacquiao renewed his rivalry with Márquez, the fierce boxer who had fought him to a controversial draw back in 2004. This time around, Pac-Man won a narrow split decision in a bout held in Las Vegas. The victory enabled him to retain the WBC and *The Ring* world super featherweight titles.

The rematch with Márquez also provided vivid evidence of the boxer's amazing popularity in his native Philippines. The bout took place at a time when the Philippine army was engaged in a bitter conflict with rebels who wanted to overthrow the government. As the hour approached for the nationally televised Pacquiao-Márquez fight, the army declared a seven-hour cease-fire so that all the troops could watch the bout. Four months after Pacquiao's victory, meanwhile, Filipinos applauded when they learned that the boxer had been selected to be the flag bearer for the Philippines at the 2008 Summer Olympics.

Pacquiao moved up yet another weight class on June 28, 2008, when he stepped into a Las Vegas ring to fight David Diaz, the WBC world lightweight champion. Some observers wondered whether Pac-Man could possibly be as effective a boxer at the heavier weight, but he quickly proved his doubters wrong. He dominated the fight, swarming Diaz with relentless attacks to claim the WBC lightweight belt. The fight ended in the ninth round, when the referee awarded Pacquiao a TKO. Afterwards, Diaz admitted that he had been overwhelmed. "I could deal with the power but not his speed," Diaz said. "His speed was uncontrollable."

On December 6, 2008, Pacquiao moved up a weight class once again to face famed U.S. welterweight Oscar De La Hoya, an Olympic gold medal winner who at one time or another had held titles in six different divisions. De La Hoya was known as one of the all-time greats, but as the match progressed it became clear that it was Pac-Man's night. He defeated De La Hoya with an eighth-round TKO. "We knew we had him after the first round," said Roach. Promoters of the Pacquiao-De La Hoya bout announced that the fight—which was the final fight in De La Hoya's tremendous career—had generated roughly $70 million in pay-per-view television revenue.

Pacquiao won a championship in a sixth weight class on May 2, 2009, when he took *The Ring's* junior welterweight title from England's Ricky Hatton. He earned this victory with a devastating second-round knockout

Pacquiao connects with a right to the head of Oscar De La Hoya during their bout in December 2008.

of Hatton in Las Vegas. Later that year, on November 14, 2009, he added another championship belt—in a record seventh weight class—when he registered a 12th-round TKO of Puerto Rican fighter Miguel Cotto to claim the WBO welterweight title.

Staying at the Top

After his loss to Pacquiao, Cotto told reporters that "Manny is one of the best boxers we have of all time." Many other people in the boxing world agreed. They pointed out that he had never failed a drug test for performance-enhancing drugs. Observers also noted that even after almost 15 years of professional boxing, he remained at the top of his game. "Pac-Man's style still features feverish punches and constant motion," Pablo S. Torre observed in *Sports Illustrated.* "The southpaw lets out a yell with every punch (Boom!) and combination (Boomboomboom!). If he takes a hard shot, he'll bang his gloves together, stick his arms into the air, and grin broadly."

Pacquiao continued his winning ways in 2010. On March 13, 2010, he defeated welterweight Joshua Clottey in a fight held before 50,000 fans at

Pacquiao battles Antonio Margarito, November 2010.

Texas Stadium in Dallas. Eight months later, on November 13, 2010, he faced Antonio Margarito for the vacant WBC world super welterweight title. Pacquiao beat Margarito so badly that the fighter was forced to spend time in the hospital for a fractured eye socket. The Margarito fight actually upset Pacquiao, who took it easy on his opponent in the later rounds because he was concerned about his health. "Instead of knocking out the guy, he asks him, 'Are you OK?'" recalled Roach. "I told him he should have knocked him out. He said, 'It's a sport, and I didn't have to hurt him; I beat him up enough.' What can you say to that?"

The victory over Margarito made Pacquiao the first boxer in history to win eight world titles in eight different boxing weight classes. Pacquiao did not keep the WBC super welterweight crown for long, though. After he decided to return to welterweight fighting, the WBC decided to leave the title open.

On May 7, 2011, Pac-Man easily defended his WBO welterweight belt against American challenger Shane Mosley, winning by unanimous decision. "He has exceptional power, power I have never been hit with before," said Mosley. But six months later, on November 12, 2011, Pacquiao barely beat his old foe Márquez in a controversial split decision. Many people who watched the fight asserted that Márquez had actually deserved the win.

Pacquiao did not agree, but he did acknowledge that his days as a professional boxer were probably drawing to a close. After all, the late 2011 bout against Márquez was his 59th professional match—and his 54th victory (he has three losses and two draws in his other five bouts). Many of the millions of people who count themselves as Pac-Man fans also recognize that the day is coming when their hero will finally hang up his gloves. They hope, however, to still be treated to another epic Pac-Man bout or two before he steps away from the ring.

A Legend in the Philippines

Pacquiao has fans all around the world, but he remains most popular in his native land. "In the Philippines," a Filipino journalist told National Public Radio, "I would say Pacquiao is like Elvis meets Justin Bieber meets Michael Jordan meets Bill Clinton." Signs of Pacquiao's stardom in the Philippines are everywhere. Posters and photos of the boxer can be found in many homes, and the Philippine government honored him by putting his image on a postage stamp. In October 2011 the Philippine military even promoted him to the position of lieutenant colonel in the Philippine Army Reserves. "Manny is our people's idol and this generation's shining light," declared Philippine President Gloria Macapagal-Arroyo in 2008. "He is our David against Goliath, our hero and the bearer of the Filipino dream.... You can feel the excitement throughout the country every time he is in the ring."

Pacquiao's tremendous popularity among his fellow Filipinos is due in large part to his boxing accomplishments, of course. His generous and playful personality is also a major factor, though. Pac-Man takes pride in being a role model for his young fans. "I never believed that you had to say bad things about your opponent to make yourself bigger," he told *USA Today.* "You can be popular, or be a champion, without trash-talking."

Pacquiao takes pride in being a role model for his young fans. "I never believed that you had to say bad things about your opponent to make yourself bigger," he said. "You can be popular, or be a champion, without trash-talking."

Pacquiao with his wife, Jinkee (left), takes his oath as Congressman of the district of Sarangani on June 28, 2010.

Pacquiao also is renowned for using his wealth to help poor individuals and communities in the Philippines. "He knows he came from nothing," explained one of his countrymen. "He knows what it is like to be poor, to beg for food and money. In the Philippines, you cannot afford to forget your roots."

In the Political Arena

Whenever Pacquiao retires from boxing, it appears that he will remain in the public eye. In early 2007 he began a second career in Filipino politics by announcing his intention to run for a seat in the Filipino House of Representatives. He actually lost his first election campaign, though. In May 2007 he was defeated by incumbent Darlene Antonino-Custodio, a wealthy and politically connected congresswoman who managed to turn her opponent's personal popularity against him. She convinced voters that Pacquiao's inspiring story might be stained if he was to get involved in the often messy business of politics.

The election-day loss surprised Pacquiao, but it did not stop him from trying again. In 2009 he formed a strong political organization to help his cause, and on May 10, 2010, he won election to represent the district of Sarangani in Congress. "I want to help people, especially in my province," he said. "There are a lot of poor people. When I'm old, I want my name, Manny Pacquiao, to be known not only as a good boxer but a good public servant."

MARRIAGE AND FAMILY

Pacquiao and his wife, Jinkee, have four children. They divide their time between big estates in General Santos City and Los Angeles.

HOBBIES AND OTHER INTERESTS

Pacquiao engages in a wide assortment of activities and hobbies. In addition to his work as a boxer and politician, he has become a major media star on Filipino television. He hosts a game show called "Manny Prizes" and even starred for a time on a sitcom called "Show Me da Manny."

Pacquiao is also famous for his love of karaoke and singing. "When I listen to music, all the stress is gone," he explained. "I feel stronger." He has recorded several hit songs in the Philippines, and in April 2011 he and songwriter Dan Hill teamed up to record a new version of Hill's 1977 hit song "Sometimes When We Touch." "The singing thing with Manny is so tender," Hill said. "This guy, such a powerful man in the ring, is unafraid to sing an emotional, sentimental song like 'Sometimes.'"

HONORS AND AWARDS

WBC (World Boxing Council) World Flyweight Champion: 1998
IBF (International Boxing Federation) World Super Bantamweight Champion: 2001
The Ring World Featherweight Champion: 2003
The Ring World Super Featherweight Champion: 2005
WBC (World Boxing Council) World Super Featherweight Champion: 2005
Fighter of the Year (Boxing Writers Association of America): 2006, 2008, 2009
Fighter of the Year (*The Ring*): 2006, 2008, 2009
Boxer of the Year (*Sports Illustrated*): 2008, 2009
Boxer of the Year (World Boxing Council): 2008, 2009
WBC (World Boxing Council) World Lightweight Champion: 2008
100 Most Influential People (*Time* Magazine): 2009
The Ring World Super Lightweight Champion: 2009
World Boxing Organization (WBO) World Welterweight Champion: 2009
ESPY Fighter of the Year (ESPN): 2009, 2011

Athlete of the Decade, 2000-2009 (Philippine Sportswriters Association): 2010

Fighter of the Decade, 2000-2009 (Boxing Writers Association of America): 2010

Fighter of the Decade, 2000-2009 (HBO): 2010

WBC (World Boxing Council) World Super Welterweight Champion: 2010

FURTHER READING

Book

Pacquiao, Manny, with Timothy James. *Pacman: My Story of Hope, Resilience, and Never-Say-Never Determination,* 2010

Periodicals

GQ, Apr. 2010

Los Angeles Times, Oct. 24, 2011; Nov. 12, 2011

Maclean's, May 23, 2011

New York Times, Sep. 18, 2010; Nov. 15, 2010; May 2, 2011; May 9, 2011

Sports Illustrated, Dec. 8, 2008, p.110; Nov. 22, 2010, p.26; May 16, 2011, p.31

Time, Nov. 16, 2009, p.44

USA Today, Nov. 12, 2010; Nov. 15, 2010; May 5, 2011; May 9, 2011

Online Articles

sports.espn.go.com
(ESPN, "All Hail the New King,"June 29, 2008; "Manny Pacquiao,"Sep. 7, 2011)

www.npr.org
(National Public Radio-NPR—All Things Considered, "Manny Pacquiao: Boxer Who Packs a Political Punch,"Feb. 16, 2011)

www.npr.org
(National Public Radio-NPR—Morning Edition, "Pacman: Last of the Great Boxers?"May 11, 2011)

ADDRESS

Manny Pacquiao
House of Representatives
Quezon City, Philippines
Rm. SWA-403, local 7952, 4424064

WEB SITES

www.mannypacquiao.com
www.mp8.ph

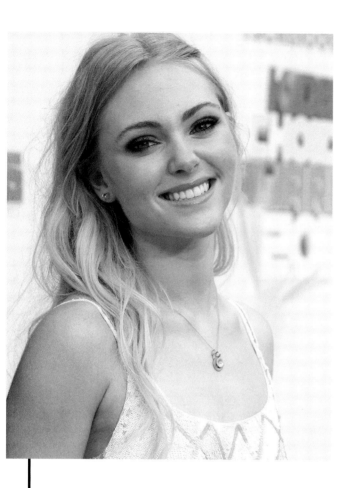

AnnaSophia Robb 1993-

American Actress
Star of the Hit Movies *Because of Winn-Dixie, Bridge to Terabithia, Charlie and the Chocolate Factory, Race to Witch Mountain,* and *Soul Surfer*

BIRTH

AnnaSophia Robb was born on December 8, 1993, in Denver, Colorado. She is the only child of Dave and Janet Robb.

YOUTH

Growing up in Denver, Robb liked gymnastics. She also liked making up stories and creating different characters to act out.

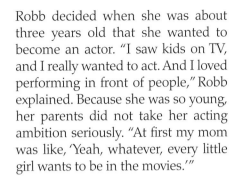

> *Robb's first acting job, in a commercial for McDonald's Happy Meals, was not the most glamorous role, but she was overjoyed at the chance to act on TV. "We ate cold french fries and old Chicken McNuggets for a really long time," she remembered. "But I thought it was just the best job ever."*

Robb decided when she was about three years old that she wanted to become an actor. "I saw kids on TV, and I really wanted to act. And I loved performing in front of people," Robb explained. Because she was so young, her parents did not take her acting ambition seriously. "At first my mom was like, 'Yeah, whatever, every little girl wants to be in the movies.'"

Robb was persistent and never wavered from her dream of becoming an actor. She was so focused on achieving her goal that she eventually convinced her parents to let her try acting. "I just love to perform. That's all I can ever remember wanting to do," she recalled. "When I was about eight, I begged my mom for an agent because that's how I heard actors got started." Her mother finally agreed. Robb got an agent and enrolled in a workshop to learn basic acting skills. After she completed the workshop, she met a producer who invited her to come to Los Angeles and try out for roles.

Robb's first trip to Los Angeles included more than 40 auditions and led to her first real acting job in a television commercial for McDonald's Happy Meals. Robb recalled that while it was not the most glamorous role, she was overjoyed at the chance to act on TV. "We ate cold french fries and old Chicken McNuggets for a really long time," she remembered. "But I thought it was just the best job ever."

EDUCATION

At first, Robb was homeschooled to accommodate her schedule of acting and going to auditions. She later enrolled in public school in Denver. Although she is often away from home while she works on movies, Robb enjoys attending public school. "I think it's important, because I want to have a regular life. It helps keep everything in perspective," she commented. "It's nice. I'm removed from the L.A. scene."

Robb's favorite subjects are current events and history. She is a member of her school's French club and the cross-country team. She studies with a tutor when she is away from home, but still stays in touch with her regular teachers in Denver. She gets assignments and turns in homework by email. Juggling schoolwork, acting, and other obligations is sometimes a challenge for Robb. "I have to have structure in my day. I need to focus on one thing or the other. I'm actually pretty bad at multi-tasking," she admitted. "Going to school, trying to do homework, trying to read a script and do interviews on the phone and all that. It's hard to balance but it's worth it."

CAREER HIGHLIGHTS

After various television commercials and smaller parts, Robb landed the title role in the 2004 television movie *Samantha: An American Girl Holiday.* She played Samantha, a character based on the popular line of American Girl dolls and books. The story takes place around the beginning of the 20th century, when nine-year-old Samantha is sent to live with relatives after the death of her parents. In her new home, she struggles with her grandmother's expectations of proper behavior and the radically different attitudes of her aunt. As she makes new friends and tries to fit in with her new family, Samantha learns about life and faces challenges she never imagined possible. For her performance as Samantha, Robb was nominated for a 2005 Young Artist Award for Best Performance in a TV Movie, Miniseries or Special—Leading Young Actress.

Because of Winn-Dixie

Robb's breakout role was in the 2005 film *Because of Winn-Dixie,* based on the Newbery Award-winning book published in 2000 by Kate DiCamillo. In this movie, Robb stars as Opal, a lonely young girl who moves to a small town with her father (played by Jeff Daniels). Her mother abandoned the family when Opal was very young, and her father refuses to talk about it. Seven years have passed since her mother left, and both Opal and her father still struggle with the loss. One day, while exploring her new town, she finds a stray dog at the supermarket. She takes him home and names him Winn-Dixie, after the store where she found him. Winn-Dixie seems to have a special influence on people, and soon Opal's father begins to tell her about her mother and the reasons why she left. As she learns about life, love, and loss, Opal realizes that she has found a new family among various townspeople, including a pet store clerk, the town librarian, and an eccentric old woman who everyone feared was a witch.

Robb remembers when she got the phone call telling her she had the part. "I started screaming! I was jumping up and screaming and running around. I was so excited because I had only been acting for about a year, and I had gotten my first big film. So I was really excited." *Because of Winn-*

Scenes from Robb's early movies:
Because of Winn-Dixie *(top)*, Samantha:
An American Girl Holiday *(middle)*,
and Charlie and the Chocolate Factory
(bottom).

Dixie pleased both moviegoers and film critics. According to Claudia Puig, a movie reviewer for *USA Today,* "What seemed to be a simple story of a girl and her dog becomes a much deeper tale about loss and companionship. But the movie doesn't moralize or dwell too long in serious emotional terrain....*Winn-Dixie* is a welcome relief: a whimsical family film about longing and belonging told with gentle humanity." Robb received a 2006 Young Artist Award nomination for Best Performance in a Feature Film (Comedy or Drama)—Leading Young Actress.

Charlie and the Chocolate Factory

In 2005, Robb appeared as Violet Beauregarde in the movie *Charlie and the Chocolate Factory.* The story is based on the 1964 book by Roald Dahl. Robb plays one of five children who win the once-in-a-lifetime opportunity to tour the mysterious and famous candy factory owned by Willy Wonka (played by Johnny Depp). At the end of the tour, one of the lucky children will be chosen to receive a special prize. Robb's character, the gum-chewing Violet, is extremely competitive, strong willed, and determined to claim the prize. But as the tour progresses, the children learn that the factory is not exactly what it appears to be, and there are surprises in store for each of them. By the end of the story, Violet and the other children learn important lessons about life and the dangers of always getting what you want.

Charlie and the Chocolate Factory was a hit with moviegoers around the world. The movie's success gave a boost to Robb's career and helped her land starring roles in her next two movies.

Bridge to Terabithia

Robb's next major role was in the 2007 movie *Bridge to Terabithia,* based on the Newbery Award-winning book published in 1977 by Katherine Paterson. In this movie, Robb plays Leslie Burke, a smart, creative, imaginative tomboy who becomes best friends with fellow loner Jess Aarons (played by Josh Hutcherson) after defeating him in a race at school. Leslie and Jess create an imaginary forest kingdom called Terabithia, which is accessible only by swinging across a creek on a rope that hangs from a tree. Jess and Leslie spend most of their free time together in Terabithia, making up stories and pretending to fight monsters. Leslie helps Jess learn about courage, strength, and true friendship. These qualities prove invaluable to Jess when he must come to terms with a terrible tragedy that he feels responsible for causing.

The movie was well regarded by movie critics and viewers. "[*Bridge to Terabithia* is] a thoughtful and extremely affecting story of a transformative

Robb and Josh Hutcherson in a scene from Bridge to Terabithia.

friendship between two unusually gifted children," wrote *New York Times* movie reviewer Jeannette Catsoulis. "Consistently smart and delicate as a spider web, *Bridge to Terabithia* is the kind of children's movie rarely seen nowadays." For her performance in *Bridge to Terabithia,* Robb was nominated for the 2008 Broadcast Film Critics Association Critics Choice Award for Best Young Actress. She won two Young Artist Awards in 2008, for Best Performance in a Feature Film—Leading Young Actress, and Best Performance in a Feature Film—Young Ensemble Cast, which she shared with her co-stars. *Bridge to Terabithia* also provided Robb with the chance to explore singing, as she recorded the song "Keep Your Mind Wide Open" for the movie's soundtrack.

Race to Witch Mountain

In 2009, Robb starred as Sara in the Disney movie *Race to Witch Mountain,* a follow up to the movies *Escape to Witch Mountain* (1975) and *Return from Witch Mountain* (1978). Sara and her brother Seth (played by Alexander Ludwig) are two otherworldly teens with paranormal powers. They are on the run from evil government agents, assassins, and scientists. They enlist the help of reluctant but heroic taxi driver Jack Bruno (played by Dwayne

Johnson, also known as The Rock), who doesn't believe in the supernatural. As the unlikely trio set off on a high-speed race to save the world, Bruno learns the truth about Sara and Seth and is forced to change his beliefs about what is real.

Race to Witch Mountain was a hit with moviegoers, although the film received mixed reviews from critics. Joe Leydon, a movie reviewer for *Variety*, noted that the film "strikes a deft balance of chase-movie suspense and wisecracking humor, with a few slam-bang action set-pieces that would shame the makers of more allegedly grown-up genre fare." Writing in the *New York Times*, reviewer A.O. Scott called *Race to Witch Mountain* "modest and diverting, rough and bland, with some good actors and so-so special effects."

Soul Surfer

Robb went on to star as Bethany Hamilton in the 2011 movie *Soul Surfer*. This film, based on Hamilton's 2004 book *Soul Surfer: A True Story of Faith, Family and Fighting to Get Back on the Board*, tells the true story of her recovery from a terrible shark attack when she was 13 years old. The story begins with the attack and its immediate aftermath, in which Hamilton lost her arm along with 60 percent of her body's blood supply. Though she was not expected to survive the massive blood loss, the story unfolds as Hamilton works to recover and adapt to living with one arm. She eventually begins surfing again, overcoming a host of challenges along the way. In her triumphant return to competitive surfing, Hamilton faces off against her arch rival in a national tournament. (For more information on Hamilton, see *Biography Today*, April 2005.)

The role proved to be a challenging and life-changing experience for Robb, who became close friends with Hamilton while making the movie. To prepare for the role, Hamilton taught Robb how to surf. "It's a really rigorous sport, but once you do it, you're kind of hooked. I've fallen in love with the ocean," she explained. She also said that she learned much more than surfing from Hamilton. "I've learned so much from her, which I'll keep with me for the rest of my life," Robb said. "It's an amazing story of the human spirit and how we can live our dream through any hardship. Bethany never felt bad for herself. She does more with one arm than I can do with two."

The movie received mixed reviews from critics. *Variety* movie reviewer Rob Nelson praised *Soul Surfer* as "a kind-hearted coming-of-age drama with killer waves." *Christianity Today* movie reviewer Carolyn Arends called Robb "strong in the central role, capturing both Bethany's resiliency and her vulnerability with natural charisma." Owen Gleiberman's comments in

Robb starred as real-life surfing champ Bethany Hamilton in Soul Surfer.

Entertainment Weekly were a bit more mixed. "*Soul Surfer,* while formulaic in design, is an authentic and heartfelt movie. At first, you think you're watching *Jaws* remade as a Miley Cyrus drama," he wrote. "But as Bethany recovers from her cataclysmic wound, AnnaSophia Robb's performance comes to life. She gives Bethany's belief in God a concrete depth and understanding. When Bethany gets up on that surfboard again, refusing to wear a prosthetic limb, her pluckiness hits home because we see that she's out to impress no one in the world but herself." For her portrayal of Hamilton in *Soul Surfer,* Robb was nominated for a 2011 Teen Choice Award.

Looking to the Future

Following the successes of her recent films, Robb plans to continue making movies that connect with audiences. "Probably one of the hardest parts, but most satisfying too, is just trying to find and create a character that's real and then just put on that character's clothes and really get into the mindset," she explained. "I try to get into the mind of my character. I have to feel what they feel, so the character is real. Good acting isn't really acting, it's 'being.'" Robb's approach to acting is based on her desire to tell stories that are meaningful, rather than purely entertaining. "Anything that's really worthy of doing and is a good script and has good people and a good director, and can help people or teach someone a lesson, I think is worth doing."

HOME AND FAMILY

Robb lives with her parents in Denver, Colorado.

HOBBIES AND OTHER INTERESTS

In her free time, Robb enjoys many different sports, including swimming, running, surfing, snowboarding, and kickboxing. She also enjoys hanging out with her friends, listening to music, and going to the movies. Robb is also committed to humanitarian work in human rights, animal rights, and environmental conservation. She works with the Dalit Freedom Network, and has traveled to India on behalf of the organization. Whenever she can, Robb tries to encourage young people to become actively involved in changing the world. She said, "Show people that you care about them because we really need to start welcoming everybody around us not just our friends and family. We need to start opening up to the world and become one community."

SELECTED CREDITS

Samantha: An American Girl Holiday, 2004
Because of Winn-Dixie, 2005

Charlie and the Chocolate Factory, 2005
Bridge to Terabithia, 2007
Race to Witch Mountain, 2009
Soul Surfer, 2011

HONORS AND AWARDS

Young Artist Award: 2008 (two awards), Best Performance in a Feature
Film—Leading Young Actress, and Best Performance in a Feature Film—
Young Ensemble Cast, shared with cast, both for *Bridge to Terabithia*

FURTHER READING

Periodicals

Current Events, Feb. 12, 2007, p.6; Mar. 28, 2011, p.6
Foam, Apr. 2011, p.33
Girls' Life, Apr./May 2009, p.48
Nylon, May 2009
Portrait, Jan. 2007
TC Magazine, Winter 2008, p.24
Teen Vogue, Apr. 2007, p.143; May 2011, p.87

Online Articles

news.christiansunite.com
(Christians Unite, "An Interview with AnnaSophia Robb, 11-Year-Old
Star of Because of *Winn-Dixie,*"Feb. 21, 2005)
www.kidzworld.com
(Kidz World, "AnnaSophia Robb Bio—Get the Look,"no date)
www.lateenfestival.com
(LA Teen Festival, "AnnaSophia Robb: A Young Star on the Move,"Issue
10)
www.radiofree.com/profiles
(Radio Free, "AnnaSophia Robb,"Feb. 5, 2007)

ADDRESS

AnnaSophia Robb
Untitled Entertainment
350 South Beverly Drive
Suite 200
Beverly Hills, CA 90212

WEB SITE

www.annasophiarobb.com

Hilda Solis 1957-

American Political Leader
Four-Term Congresswoman from California
U.S. Secretary of Labor

BIRTH

Hilda Lucia Solis was born on October 20, 1957, in Los Angeles, California. She was the third child born to Raul Solis and Juana Sequiera Solis. She has four sisters and two brothers.

YOUTH

Solis's parents were both immigrants to the United States. Her father was born in Mexico, where he worked in a shop and was active with a labor union. (Labor unions are organizations created to make sure that workers get fair pay and treatment.) Upon coming to the United States, he settled in the Los Angeles area and began working at a plant where batteries were recycled. He became a member of the International Brotherhood of Teamsters, the union that served workers at the plant. He was active in the union's struggle to get better health care for employees.

Solis's mother had a similar story. Born in Nicaragua, she also headed north in search of a better quality of life. She found work at a toy factory near Los Angeles, where she worked shifts as long as 10 hours. She joined the United Rubber Workers Union and was outspoken about the poor working conditions at the factory. She and her husband met during classes they had to take in order to attain U.S. citizenship.

> *Solis's father taught his children "to stand up for your rights, and regardless of who you are and where you come from, to hold your head up high with dignity and respect."*

Solis believes that her family benefited greatly from her parents' membership in the unions. Without protection from the unions, both of her parents probably would have been fired for their efforts to improve working conditions. Furthermore, the unions ensured that they were paid decently and received good benefits. Therefore, even though they came to the United States with very little, they were able to save some of the money they worked so hard to earn. They purchased a home in La Puenta, a working-class area just east of the city of Los Angeles.

La Puenta represented security and upward mobility for the Solis family, yet it was also an area with many problems. Many residents were unemployed and lacked adequate housing. Everyone in the area suffered from the effects of significant air and water pollution. The Puente Hills Landfill, a gigantic landfill some 22 stories deep, sat over the water table that supplied the region. If the wind blew in the right direction, the stench from the landfill was easy to smell at the Solis home. The pollution from this landfill inspired Solis's later work to protect the poor from environmental toxins. The Puente Hills Landfill is still in operation today and is currently the largest active landfill in the United States, taking in more than 10,000 tons of garbage a day.

The Solis family was better off than many in La Puenta, but life was not easy. Hilda Solis had to grow up quickly. When she was ten years old, her

Solis grew up near the Puenta Hills Landfill, the largest active landfill in the United States and the source of a tremendous amount of pollution in East LA and the surrounding area.

mother had twins and had to return to an overnight shift at her factory job soon afterwards. Solis was the one in charge of the infant twins and her other younger siblings when her mother was out. She developed a mature, serious attitude at a young age. She remembered her father telling his children how important it was "to stand up for your rights, and regardless of who you are and where you come from, to hold your head up high with dignity and respect."

EDUCATION

Solis attended La Puenta High School. Her counselor there tried to steer her away from college, telling her she should consider becoming a secretary instead, but Solis disregarded that advice. After graduating from La Puenta High, she enrolled at California State Polytechnic University. With the help of government funding, she became the first person in her family to attend college. In addition to her studies, she also worked as an interpreter for the Immigration and Naturalization Service. In 1979, she graduated with a Bachelor of Arts degree (BA) in political science. She then entered a master's program at the University of Southern California (USC) to study public administration.

While working on her master's degree, Solis was determined to get some experience in the nation's capitol. She sent out about 100 letters inquiring

―――― " ――――

"There are so many people I knew when I was growing up who were not even paid the minimum wage," Solis recalled. "People wouldn't know where to go to lodge a complaint. And if you didn't speak good English, forget it."

―――― " ――――

about internships with various federal agencies in Washington, DC. Her efforts paid off: she was offered a job working for President Jimmy Carter in the White House Office of Hispanic Affairs. There, she gained valuable experience in the way government works and also got a broader perspective about what life was like for Latinos beyond the Los Angeles area.

The experience of working for the Carter administration was very important to Solis. A classmate of hers who also worked for Carter at that time said, "I think being at the White House empowered her to say: 'You can do anything you want to do if you work hard.'" Solis completed her studies at the University of Southern California and earned her Master of Public Administration degree (MPA) in 1981.

FIRST JOBS

In 1981 President Jimmy Carter, a Democrat, left office, and Ronald Reagan, a Republican, became president. During a change in administration like this, many staffers lose their jobs as the new president brings in his own team. Solis was asked to stay on in Washington, working as an analyst in the Office of Management and Budget. She accepted the position, but only a few months passed before she found herself uncomfortable with the conservative Republican politics of the Reagan administration. She left the job and returned to California.

Back in her home state, Solis returned to the area around eastern Los Angeles, where she lived and worked throughout her political career. She also turned her attention to education, becoming director of the California Student Opportunity and Access Program in 1982. This organization helps disadvantaged youths to prepare for college. In 1984, she won her first elected position when she was voted in as a member of the Rio Hondo Community College board of trustees. She was re-elected in 1989. While on the board at Rio Hondo, Solis worked to upgrade the quality of the college's vocational training and to increase the number of women and minority members on the faculty.

In 1991, Solis was named a commissioner on the Los Angeles County Commission on Insurance. She was appointed to the position by Gloria

As a California state senator, Solis fought for the rights of workers.
She helped to investigate an illegal garment factory in El Monte
that enslaved these workers, and others, from Thailand.

Molina, the Los Angeles County Supervisor. Molina was a powerful political mentor who could help advance her career. Solis also gained valuable experience working as chief of staff for Art Torres, a California state senator.

CAREER HIGHLIGHTS

Serving in the California State Legislature

In 1992, Solis was elected to the California State Assembly. Her family gave her support on the most basic level—her mom even cooked burritos for the volunteers working on her campaign. One of her first actions in the assembly was to vote for legislation that made it illegal to smoke in any California workplace. By doing that, she sent a clear signal that she wasn't afraid to take a stand against big-business interests, including the tobacco industry.

In 1994, Solis became the first Latina to be elected to the California State Senate. As a senator, she increased her reputation as a hard worker and as a staunch labor supporter. She was also named the chairwoman of the Senate Industrial Relations Committee. Not long after she took office, state authorities discovered an illegal garment factory operating in El Monte, California. Inside, 72 people from Thailand were being held in terrible conditions and forced to work. Solis gave her support to a very thorough investigation of the matter that led to much better enforcement of the laws protecting garment workers.

In 1996, Solis supported legislation that raised California's minimum wage from $4.25 to $5.75 an hour. Her background helped her feel sympathy for people who work for low wages and for those who are easy victims of employers who want to exploit them. Solis wanted to protect these workers. "There are so many people I knew when I was growing up who were not even paid the minimum wage," she recalled. "People wouldn't know where to go to lodge a complaint. And if you didn't speak good English, forget it."

This pro-labor, pro-worker stance did not make Solis popular with everyone. Big business interests sometimes view workers' rights and protections as barriers to higher profits. Even those politicians who did not agree with her thought highly of her, however. "We obviously didn't see eye to eye," said Rob Hurtt, a conservative senator who served at the same time as Solis. "But she was respectful. I'll give her credit; she was a very hard worker and she knew her stuff."

Working for Environmental Justice

The voters liked Solis and reelected her to the California senate in 1998. The following year, she was the author of Senate Bill 115, a bill that defined the term "environmental justice." Environmental justice refers to the fact that environmental problems disproportionately affect poor people and people of color. People in poor areas are much more likely to be the victims of toxic waste dumping and other forms of pollution than are people in more well-to-do areas. For example, Solis's district was home to 17 gravel pits and numerous abandoned gas stations, both of which can cause significant pollution; 5 landfills; 4 Superfund sites, which are places polluted with particularly toxic substances, eligible for federal funding for cleanup; and the San Gabriel Basin, which is one of the most polluted water sources in the United States.

Senate Bill 115 was the first of its kind to be signed into law. It required the California Environmental Protection Agency to adopt environmental justice standards, and it paved the way for more such laws to be written and passed. Because of her work for environmental justice, Solis was honored with the John F. Kennedy Profile in Courage Award in 2000. She was the first woman ever to receive the prestigious award. In a statement released by the John F. Kennedy Library, she was praised for her willingness to take on "entrenched economic interests as she sought relief for minority communities that suffered the ill effects of haphazard enforcement of environmental laws." Solis gave the $25,000 cash portion of the prize to environmental groups in her area.

Serving in the U.S. House of Representatives

Solis's advocacy for workers, unions, and the environment had made her a favorite of the voters in her district. In 2000, she decided to run in the primary election for a seat in the U.S. House of Representatives, representing the 31st Congressional District. (District boundaries were later redefined, and then she represented the 32nd District.) Running for the U.S. House of Representatives meant she was challenging incumbent Democrat Matthew G. Martinez, who had held the office for nine terms. Some people in the community felt that Solis was being disrespectful by challenging the long-established congressman. Yet others felt that Martinez was out of touch with district voters and their needs. While the Democratic Party wouldn't endorse Solis's challenge to Martinez, she did win the support of many key people in the Latino community. She beat Martinez decisively in the primary, with a winning margin of 69 to 31 percent. With no Republican challenger in the general election, she won that contest as well and returned to Washington, DC as a member of the U.S. Congress.

Solis's main goals in Congress were the improvement of access to affordable health care for all workers, safeguarding the environment, improving the lives of working families, and protecting immigrants' rights. She was known to be closely allied with Nancy Pelosi, another Democratic congresswoman from California who was also the Speaker of the House. Solis served in many special capacities. She was chair of the Congressional Hispanic Caucus Task Force on Health and the Environment and co-chair of the Congressional Women's Caucus. She was a member of numerous important committees, including the House Natural Resources Committee, the House Energy and Commerce Committee, the Education and the Workforce Committee, and the

"People have to be reminded that unions played a very historic role in our economy," Solis asserted. *"If you didn't have unions, you wouldn't have Saturdays and Sundays [off]; you wouldn't be paid a minimum wage, be guaranteed paid overtime and sick leave and a pension. Believe it or not, we still have these issues come up."*

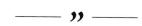

In a show of labor support, U.S. Congresswoman Solis adds her name to a display expressing support for hotel workers who were negotiating a union contract.

House Select Committee on Energy Independence and Global Warming. She was reelected in 2002, 2004, 2006, and 2008.

Throughout her time in Congress, Solis consistently worked for the good of the environment and for job creation and workers' rights. She was considered both idealistic and tough. In 2003, she helped to start a federal study about how to conserve the health of the water sources in her district. In 2005, she voiced her opposition to the Central American Free Trade Agreement (CAFTA). She compared it to the North American Free Trade Agreement (NAFTA), which in her words, resulted in "750,000 jobs lost in the United States and little progress in improving workers' rights in Mexico." In 2007, she lent her support to the Green Jobs Act, which was intended to train workers for environmentally friendly work.

Becoming Secretary of Labor

During the primary elections leading up to the 2008 presidential election, the race for who would become the Democratic candidate for president gradually narrowed down to two candidates: Barack Obama and Hillary Clinton. Solis was a strong supporter of Clinton, who lost the race to Obama. When Obama was nominated as the Democratic candidate, he immediately asked for Solis's support for his campaign. Her endorsement of his candidacy was seen as a very important factor in winning the Latino vote. After he won the presidential election, Obama nominated Solis as Secretary of Labor on December 18, 2008. She recalled Obama telling her that if she took the job, he wanted her to be "the voice for working families and organized labor."

There was little opposition to her nomination, and on February 24, 2009, Solis was confirmed by the Senate as the U.S. Secretary of Labor. As such she became part of the Cabinet, the group of the president's top advisors who lead the major departments of the U.S. government. Solis was the first Latina to serve in the Cabinet. Upon taking office, she assumed responsibility for making sure laws regulating safe working conditions were enforced and companies that broke them were penalized. She also took responsibility for the Department of Labor's $10.5 billion budget (now about $12.8 billion). It

———— **"** ————

Solis brings a methodical approach to her work, according to a former professor who has known her since her college days. "[Solis is] a person who is very organized, who will lay out a plan of action, and quietly carry it through. I think that's what has made her effective: She's not a show-boat person, she's not a talker. ... And she does things without grandstanding it, she does things quietly."

———— **"** ————

was a difficult time to be the Secretary of Labor. The economy was troubled and unemployment was very high. Nevertheless, Solis brought a positive attitude to her new position and a commitment to finding ways to create new jobs and continuing to protect the rights of workers.

When Obama was elected president, he succeeded George W. Bush, whose policies had been strongly pro-business. Solis felt that during the Bush administration the Department of Labor had been neglected, or even restrained from carrying out key parts of its mission to protect workers. Almost as soon as she took office, she declared herself the "new sheriff in town" and set out to establish a high standard for workplace safety.

In her first year alone, Solis took the following actions: she hired 250 new workplace inspectors to ensure safety rules were being followed; she increased funding to the U.S. Occupational Safety and Health Administration (OSHA), a governmental agency that exists to ensure worker safety; and she imposed a huge fine on BP, a large and powerful oil company, for

—— " ——

"As the first Latina to serve in a U.S. President's cabinet, I am committed to ensuring that the nation's Latino communities are part of America's effort to outcompete the world," Solis stated. *"Achieving that requires good communication, and ensuring that Latinos have the information they need to do their jobs safely, provide for their families, and share in the country's economic recovery."*

—— " ——

violations of safety regulations that took place in 2005, before she was in office. At $87 million, the fine was four times larger than any that had ever been previously imposed by the Department of Labor. It came in response to BP's failure to make repairs that were needed at a Texas oil refinery. BP failed to maintain and repair equipment at the refinery, investigators found, which caused a massive explosion that killed 15 people and injured 170. Solis wanted to send a message that workers were more important than any company's profits. "An $87 million fine won't restore those lives, but we can't let this happen again," she stated.

Solis supported the Employee Free Choice Act (EFCA), a piece of legislation that was designed to make it easier for workers to form unions. Big business interests generally disliked EFCA, while labor interests considered it vital. One of the more controversial aspects of EFCA was the "card check" measure. This would have forced employers to officially recognize the existence of a union once more than half of its employees signed cards indicating their support. Yet even some Democrats disliked the card check measure, saying it made it impossible for employees to remain anonymous about whether or not they had voted to unionize. In July 2009, the card check provision was written out of EFCA, but the act still found little support in Congress.

On April 5, 2010, Solis faced her first significant workplace disaster as Secretary of Labor. At the Upper Big Branch Mine in West Virginia, an explosion occurred about 1,000 feet underground. Despite rescue efforts, 29 of the 31 miners working at the site lost their lives. It was the worst mining accident to occur in the United States since 1970. Solis went to Upper Big Branch herself to inspect conditions and do whatever she could help rescue operations. "In times like these, one thinks two things: First, why is this even happening?" she asked. "Mine accidents are preventable. No

President Barack Obama looks at a map of the Upper Big Branch Mine during a meeting in the Oval Office on mine safety with Solis and top staffers.

one should have to go through all this. And second: What more could we have done?"

Reaching Out

The Department of Labor is entrusted with the safety and well-being of all U.S. workers. But Solis is particularly interested in reaching out to groups who find themselves on the fringes of mainstream society, including the Latino community. In March 2011, the Latino news and information company impreMedia announced that Solis would be featured in a monthly column distributed by their service, called "Tu Trabajo." It would function as a forum where Latino audiences could ask questions and learn about programs and services available to them through the Department of Labor. "As the first Latina to serve in a U.S. President's cabinet, I am committed to ensuring that the nation's Latino communities are part of America's effort to outcompete the world," Solis stated "Achieving that requires good communication, and ensuring that Latinos have the information they need to do their jobs safely, provide for their families, and share in the country's economic recovery."

Solis put the Department of Labor to work for many other marginalized segments of society as well. For example, in July 2011 she announced that

> "Getting Americans back to work, expanding opportunities, ensuring the safety of workers, and protecting their right to keep what they earn—these are all top priorities for my department," Solis said.

$20 million in grants would be made available to prisoners being released from jail. Ex-convicts often have a hard time readjusting to life outside prison and have a harder-than-average time finding work. As a result, they often end up drifting back into crime and returning to jail. The Department of Labor grants funded programs that help ex-convicts succeed at their jobs and function well in society. The program makes good economic sense as well as humanitarian sense, Solis pointed out. Studies have shown that workers who have been in jail tend to value their jobs more highly because they know it is difficult for them to find employment. They have been shown to work harder and be more productive than many workers who have not done jail time. If they succeed as working members of society, they will not end up costing taxpayers money by needing to be on welfare or living in homeless shelters.

In September 2011, Solis revealed a plan to spend $2.2 million on the "Add Us In" initiative. The goal of Add Us In is to open up more job opportunities for disabled people by helping businesses and communities find ways to make jobs more accessible for the disabled. This is important because the unemployment rate is significantly higher for disabled people than for those who are not disabled.

In the following month, Solis announced that $32.5 million would be spent on grants to fight child labor internationally. On the same day that news was made public, the Department of Labor also released three reports detailing the situation on child labor around the world. More than 215 million children are believed to be used as forced labor around the world, and more them half of those children are engaged in dangerous work. Solis stated her belief that with "increased education and awareness, and critical assistance to families and governments, we can help make exploitative child labor a thing of the past." Solis also hosted a panel discussion on child labor and how to fight it, bringing together authorities on the subject from around the world.

On the matter of illegal immigration, Solis believes it is wrong to focus only on stern enforcement of existing laws to keep immigrants out. She feels it is vital to take a more realistic and humanitarian approach to the

Secretary of Labor Solis meets with an autoworker while touring a Jeep plant in Toledo, Ohio.

problem, one that takes into consideration the hardships endured by these immigrants and their families. She believes this can be done without endangering national security. She has stated her belief that "immigrant workers should be documented, allowing them to enjoy the rights and to exercise the responsibilities of U.S. citizens. We can heighten national security while bringing millions of hard-working immigrants out of the shadows and into full citizenship. But first we have to give up the illusion that enforcement alone can solve our immigration crisis."

Creating Jobs and Protecting Workers

As Secretary of Labor, Solis brings a methodical approach to her work, according to a former professor who has known her since her college days. "Hilda is not a very extroverted person; she's the kind of person who is a very methodical plotter, in the best sense of the word, not 'plotter' in the sense of conspiracy. But, a person who is very organized, who will lay out a plan of action, and quietly carry it through. I think that's what has made her effective: She's not a show-boat person, she's not a talker, she's a kind of person that does. And she does things without grandstanding it, she does things quietly."

Solis has said that when she accepted the position as Secretary of Labor, she really did not understand just how important the job was. She has found that she has much more influence than she expected to have. "Getting Americans back to work, expanding opportunities, ensuring the safety of workers, and protecting their right to keep what they earn—these are all top priorities for my department," she said. She emphasized the vital role the Department of Labor plays in protecting workers. "We take for granted much of what we have, and if we erode those protections, we're going to see more casualties and more fatalities. People have to be reminded that unions played a very historic role in our economy. If you didn't have unions, you wouldn't have Saturdays and Sundays [off]; you wouldn't be paid a minimum wage, be guaranteed paid overtime and sick leave and a pension. Believe it or not, we still have these issues come up."

HOME AND FAMILY

Solis met Sam H. Sayyad while living in Washington, DC when she was working on her master's degree. They married in June 1982. Sayyad owns an auto-repair shop not far from their home in El Monte, California. They have no children. Solis is Roman Catholic.

HOBBIES AND OTHER INTERESTS

Solis has very little free time, but she enjoys salsa dancing when she gets the chance. She also enjoys riding her bike, taking her nieces and nephews to Disneyland, and listening to music, especially jazz.

HONORS AND AWARDS

John F. Kennedy Profile in Courage Award (John F. Kennedy Library Foundation): 2000
Distinguished Public Health Legislator of the Year Award (American Public Health Association): 2007

FURTHER READING

Periodicals

Current Biography Yearbook, 2009
Hispanic, June 2000, p.20
National Journal, Sep. 10, 2010
Sierra, June 2004, p.44

Online Articles

articles.latimes.com
    (Los Angeles Times, "Hilda Solis' Belief in Unions Runs Deep," Jan. 9, 2009, and "Patt Morrison Asks: U.S. Secretary of Labor Hilda Solis," Sep. 3, 2011)

www.nytimes.com
(New York Times, Steven Greenhouse, "As Labor Secretary, Finding In-
fluence in Her Past," July 5, 2009)
www.nytimes.com/pages/topics/
(New York Times, multiple articles, various dates)
www.time.com
(Time, "Labor Secretary: Hilda Solis," Dec. 22, 2008)
www.usnews.com
(U.S. News and World Report, "10 Things You Didn't Know about Hilda
Solis," Feb. 13, 2009)
usatoday.com
(USA Today, Hilda Solis, "There Are Jobs Out There," Sep. 3, 2010)
www.washingtonpost.com
(Washington Post, "People in the News: Hilda L. Solis, Secretary of
Labor," no date)
www.washingtonpost.com/whorunsgov
(Washington Post, WhoRunsGov, "Hilda Solis," no date)

ADDRESS

Hilda Solis
U.S. Department of Labor
Frances Perkins Building
200 Constitution Ave., NW
Washington, DC 20210

WEB SITES

www.dol.gov/_sec
www.allgov.com/Official/Solis__Hilda
www.facebook.com/hildasolis

Rita Williams-Garcia 1957-
American Author of Novels for Young Adults
Winner of the 2011 Coretta Scott King Award for
One Crazy Summer

BIRTH

Rita Williams-Garcia was born Rita Williams on April 13, 1957, in Queens, New York. Her father, James Williams, had a career in the army and served in the Vietnam War for two years. Her mother, Essie Williams, was a domestic servant who volunteered with an anti-poverty program during the Vietnam War era. Williams-Garcia has an older brother, Russell Williams, and an older sister, Rosalind Rogers.

YOUTH

Williams-Garcia spent her early years in an apartment in Far Rockaway, a neighborhood in the Queens borough of New York City. Because of her father's military obligations, the family moved eight times before she was 12 years old. They lived in Arizona, California, and Georgia before eventually moving back to Jamaica, New York, a predominantly African-American neighborhood in Queens.

Williams-Garcia had few toys when she was young but remembers playing with wooden alphabet blocks frequently, which contributed to her early interest in words. She also engaged in imaginative play and told herself stories to pass the time. She was a very observant child, teaching herself to read at an early age by looking at billboards, cereal boxes, and her sister's textbooks. "My mother discovered I could read when we went to the Red Cross for our shots," she explained. "I knew all of the letters on the eye chart and could produce their sounds. When I figured out the sounds made words and the words made pictures—well, at two and a half, I was hooked." By age four she was writing adventure stories and nursery rhymes.

> **"My siblings and I indulged in now-vanishing pastimes," Williams-Garcia recalled. "We played hard. Read books. Colored with crayons. Rode bikes. Spoke as children spoke. Dreamed our childish dreams. If our parents did anything for us at all, they gave us a place to be children and kept the adult world in its place—as best as they could."**

Williams-Garcia has shared many fond memories of growing up in Seaside, California, where she spent countless hours playing kickball, roller skating, and "dirt clod fighting" outdoors. "My siblings and I indulged in now-vanishing pastimes," she recalled. "We played hard. Read books. Colored with crayons. Rode bikes. Spoke as children spoke. Dreamed our childish dreams. If our parents did anything for us at all, they gave us a place to be children and kept the adult world in its place—as best as they could." Her parents had firm rules and high expectations for their children, providing a home environment that the author has described as "a safe place for us to dream and achieve." They also instilled in them a sense of social responsibility. For example, Rita and her siblings would come to the rescue of kids who were bullied at school or in the neighborhood.

Williams-Garcia has cited her mother, known as Miss Essie, as the most influential figure in her life, crediting her as an artistic inspiration. "She frightened me, made me laugh, and loved to paint things in weird colors— napalm orange, chartreuse, and aqua. She encouraged me to be creative and to see objects and situations beyond their physicality," the author explained. In addition to Miss Essie's creative spirit, Williams-Garcia has also discussed her mother's strength of character and no-nonsense parenting style, which included physical punishment. "My mother was clear about do's and don'ts, so you couldn't plead ignorance or miscommunication. Miss Essie was quite the communicator," she stated.

In 1969, when Williams-Garcia was 12 years old, the family left California for Georgia. After six months in the South, they moved back to Queens, settling in the neighborhood of Jamaica. She recalls experiencing culture shock during this transition. "We had no backyard to play in, no great outdoors," she revealed. "School was hardly a safe-haven. Fighting for the underdog became a thing of the past. We learned quickly to mind our own business. During those times, my journal became my confidant. I wrote in it faithfully." Her love for words grew as she entered adolescence, and she grew hungry for literature featuring female African-American protagonists. At the time, she found only the books *Mary Ellen, Student Nurse* and *Amos Fortune, Free Man,* both of which she enjoyed. Wanting more, however, she read the biographies of two important historical figures: Sojourner Truth, a slave who escaped and became an abolitionist and women's rights activist, and Harriet Tubman, an escaped slave who helped other slaves find freedom along the Underground Railroad.

Around the same time, Williams-Garcia developed the habit of jotting down story ideas in a notebook throughout the day. In the evening, after she had completed her homework, she would write at least 500 words of her continuing autobiographical novel. She also kept a diary. "I laugh when I read my early work," she said, "but writing it developed my writing rhythm. It helped that writing was my own thing and I looked forward to doing it." In seventh grade she began spending afternoons and weekends in the library reading *The Writer's Market, The Writer's Handbook,* and other guides on how to get published. She mailed out a manuscript every week to publishers and quickly accumulated a stack of rejection letters. When she was 14, however, her hard work began to pay off—she sold her first story to *Highlights* magazine and her second to *Essence* when she was a college student.

EDUCATION

As a student, Williams-Garcia was very conscientious and always eager to demonstrate her knowledge. In elementary school, this self-described

Williams-Garcia working at her writing desk.

geek would often spend her recess time writing stories and poems. "I was a proud little nerd with my hands clasped on my desk ready to rocket in the air when the teacher asked a question. My classmates wanted to kill me," she joked.

Williams-Garcia attended Hofstra University in New York, determined to try new things—eating liver, scheduling a dental appointment, and taking dance classes. She soon became a serious dancer studying under choreographers Alvin Ailey and Phil Black. "I had a gift for dance but was too shy to pursue it in high school," she admitted. "Before long I was taking classes in school, then jumping on the LIRR [train] to take classes at Alvin Ailey's and Phil Black's in Manhattan. I lived in leotards."

Another new thing Williams-Garcia decided to try was studying economics. "I truly believed blacks needed to have an active role in the distribution of capital within their communities, and I planned to be at the forefront of this movement," she remembered. For three years, she temporarily abandoned writing in favor of other activities, including political activism, a leadership role in a dance company, and community outreach with her sorority, Alpha Kappa Alpha. She eventually changed her academic focus, graduating from Hofstra in 1980 with a Bachelor of Arts degree (BA) in liberal arts.

During her senior year, Williams-Garcia took a fiction workshop led by noted authors Richard Price and Sonia Pilcer, which revived her interest in creative writing. At the same time, she was involved in a volunteer tutoring initiative to help high school girls who were reading below their grade level. She combined her writing ambitions with her outreach work to produce a draft of what would become her first novel, *Blue Tights*. She created her protagonist, Joyce, in an effort to awaken the girls to a love of reading. "Contemporary urban black girls were hard to find in literature in the early 80s," she explained. "They weren't non-existent—just hard to find. Honestly, if I had found Alice Childress or Rosa Guy's novels, *Blue Tights* wouldn't have been written.... Since I couldn't find the right book to speak to a group of girls I worked with in college, I came up with Joyce, her big butt and low self-esteem. The girls in my group didn't want to read about a victimized, heroic girl or a 'good' girl. They wanted a real girl. They wanted to identify."

"I was born to write stories," Williams-Garcia said. *"When I'm not working, I'm daydreaming. Plotting out the next story. Listening to understand my character."*

In the early 1990s Williams-Garcia went back to school part-time to pursue a graduate degree. In 1997 she earned a Master of Arts degree (MA) in creative writing from Queens College. "I can't tell you how I balanced writing, my job, school, and family," she said of her graduate school experience. "None of these things are possible without the support and understanding of my family."

CAREER HIGHLIGHTS

Blue Tights

After finishing her bachelor's degree in 1980, Williams-Garcia planned "to take my manuscript, get an agent, sell it, find an island, and write the Pulitzer Prize-winning novel." In the meantime, she took a clerical job in the mailroom of a marketing software company in Manhattan and sent out her manuscript—*Blue Tights, Big Butt*—to various publishers, only to receive a pile of rejection letters. Editors noted that the main character was not a positive role model and was overly concerned with her physical appearance. Despite these criticisms, she continued to try to sell her novel for three years before tucking it away. She meanwhile accepted a new job within her firm as a promotional writer, married Peter Garcia, and started a family.

In the mid-1980s the marketing firm eliminated her writing position, and Williams-Garcia took an administrative job within the company. Deciding

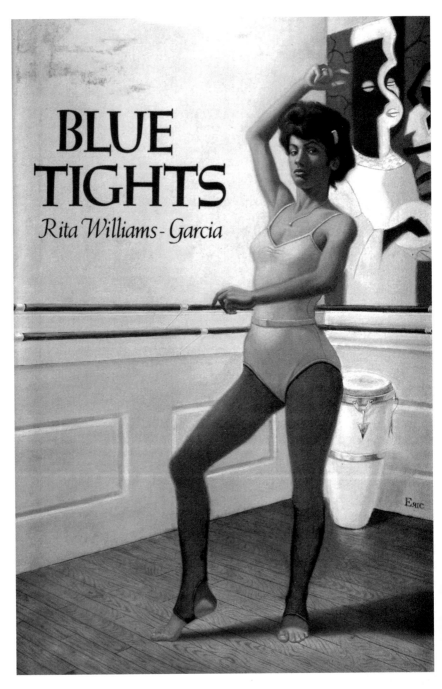

Williams-Garcia worked on her first novel, Blue Tights,
for almost 10 years before it was published.

it was time to write again, she dusted off her manuscript, made some revisions, and looked for publishers who might be interested in realistic depictions of adolescence. She sent a query letter to Rosemary Brosnan of Lodestar Books that asked: "What would you do if … your ballet teacher tells you your butt's too big for *Swan Lake*?" Brosnan was immediately intrigued. She met with Williams-Garcia in 1986 to discuss a revision strategy and then guided her through an extensive editing process. "Blue Tights needed work," Brosnan admitted in *Horn Book Magazine*, "but there was something about it that was clearly unique, and the author had a fresh, vibrant voice."

Blue Tights was published in 1988 and received a warm welcome by reviewers. The novel follows the life of Joyce Collins, a voluptuous 15-year-old with a gift for dance, as she struggles with self-esteem and her place within her family and urban community. After her ballet teacher remarks that she does not have a dancer's body, she joins an African-American troupe that accepts her for who she is, which allows her to achieve success and independence. *Blue Tights* won several awards and was a hit with critics, who remarked on the novel's uplifting ending, powerful subject matter, and believable characters. As Rudine Sims Bishop stated in *Horn Book Magazine*, "Williams-Garcia has created in Joyce a credible teenager—headstrong, confused, self-absorbed, but capable of positive growth and change. Young-adult readers will recognize something of themselves and appreciate the honesty of her story."

Writing for Young Adults

Williams-Garcia did not start off intending to write for a teenage audience. In contrast, she idolized authors Toni Morrison and Alice Walker, and she hoped to write postmodern fiction for adults. When she told Brosnan that *Blue Tights* would be her last young adult novel, she truly meant it. That changed, however, when the idea for another character came to her. "I was born to write stories," she said. "When I'm not working, I'm daydreaming. Plotting out the next story. Listening to understand my character." As it turned out, that next character was also an African-American teen, and the author has since come to view writing for young people as her passion and her mission. "I find young people interesting. They have such potential," she stated. "Their thoughts and actions matter and have great consequences. There is nothing simple about their lives, which makes for fertile ground."

Williams-Garcia was inspired to write her next book after she ran into an acquaintance from school, a young man who was now working at a fast-food restaurant. He had dropped out of college despite showing a lot of potential. This encounter prompted her to write *Fast Talk on a Slow Track* for "those bright young men who couldn't accept failure as a part of learning." The novel is about Denzel Watson, a class valedictorian who has breezed through high school and is headed to Princeton. Facing potential failure for the first time, he opts to attend community college instead, where he knows he can pass with minimal effort. Although he is not portrayed as an honorable character, the reader comes to understand that he is struggling with self-doubt. After getting a taste for life on the street by selling candy door-to-door, he ultimately decides to study at Princeton. The book was published in 1991 to positive reviews and was named a Best Book for Young Adults by the American Library Association.

Williams-Garcia's next work, *Like Sisters on the Homefront* (1995), is considered her breakthrough novel. "Of all my books, I believe *Like Sisters on the Homefront* was the story that I enjoyed telling," she stated. "I knew it would have profound meaning for my readers.... They have all connected with the characters and the story." The novel centers on 14-year-old Gayle, who becomes pregnant with her second child. At her mother's insistence, Gayle undergoes an abortion and is sent to Georgia to live with her Uncle Luther, a minister, and his family. While there, Gayle grows very close to her great-grandmother, whose strong will and stubbornness mirror her own. Critics hailed the book for its authentic dialect, memorable characters, and dynamic narrative style. It was featured on the recommended reading lists of *School Library Journal, Publishers Weekly,* and the American Library Association, among other organizations, and it received an honorable mention from the Coretta Scott King Award committee. In 1997 Williams-Garcia garnered the PEN/Norma Klein Award for a New Children's Fiction Writer in recognition of her first three books.

After publishing her first picture book, *Catching the Wild Waiyuuzee* (2000), to favorable reviews, Williams-Garcia returned to writing for an adolescent audience with *Every Time a Rainbow Dies* (2001). The story centers on Thulani, a shy 16-year-old boy who witnesses a rape. He intervenes on the victim's behalf and eventually falls in love with her. The book received a warm reception from critics. "Well-observed and subtle, Williams-Garcia's latest novel artfully interplays harsh urban realities with adolescent innocence," wrote Nell D. Beram in *Horn Book Magazine.* The American Library Association included *Every Time A Rainbow Dies* on its Top 10 Best Books for Young Adults in 2002.

Williams-Garcia's next book, *No Laughter Here* (2004), tackles sensitive subject matter through the eyes of fifth-graders Akilah and Victoria, the latter of whom has just returned from a summer in Nigeria. Victoria's fami-

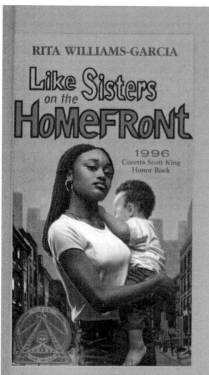

The award-winning novel
Like Sisters on the Homefront
*(top); and Williams-Garcia working
with a high school student who is
sharing a graphic novel version of
the same book (bottom).*

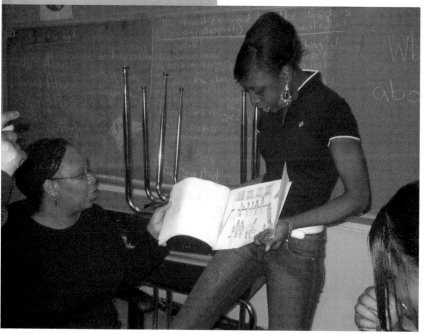

ly made the trip to her birthplace for what they described as a "special celebration to mark her coming of age." While there, she undergoes female genital mutilation, a cultural practice prevalent in some parts of Africa. During this procedure, part or all of the external female genitalia is removed. Many major groups, including the World Health Organization, the United Nations Commission on Human Rights, and the American Medical Association, have called for an end to this practice, which has zero health benefits and can cause serious physical complications. According to the World Health Organization, 100 to 140 million females worldwide are currently living with the consequences of genital mutilation. *No Laughter Here* demonstrates how the trauma of this procedure has affected Victoria, whose once-sparkling personality has faded to the point that she barely speaks. A commentator for *Kirkus Reviews* called the novel "unapologetic, fresh, and painful," and other reviewers admired the grace and skill with which Williams-Garcia related this powerful and delicate narrative.

> ——— **"** ———
>
> *"I find young people interesting. They have such potential," Williams-Garcia stated. "Their thoughts and actions matter and have great consequences. There is nothing simple about their lives, which makes for fertile ground."*
>
> ——— **"** ———

In 2005 Williams-Garcia left her day job to concentrate on writing full-time. After 25 years of writing during her subway commute and on her lunch hour, she suddenly had significantly more time to devote to her craft. "There's something to be said for finally being in the life you were meant to have," she affirmed. "I write every day except for Sunday." Despite having more time, Williams-Garcia has said that her next novel, *Jumped* (2009), was the hardest to write. "Getting through *Jumped* was a trek through the desert. I thought I'd have this thing wrapped up in six months, tops. It took two years to submit the manuscript to my most patient editor," she lamented. "*Jumped* went through editing and was placed on the publisher's calendar for release two years later. So altogether, it's been four years from spark to print.... So many drafts. So many restarts."

Jumped addresses the issue of female-initiated peer violence and the idea of bystander responsibility. Narrated from the varying perspectives of its three central characters, the novel documents the events of a school day during which Leticia overhears Dominique threaten to beat up Trina after school. Leticia must decide whether or not to get involved in the conflict between the angry tough girl and the oblivious pretty girl. Critics noted the author's well-observed characterizations and the lingering impact of her message. "Teens will relate to Leticia's dilemma even as they may criticize her motives, and the ethical decision she faces will get readers thinking about the larger issues surrounding community, personal responsibility, and the concept of 'snitching,'" noted Meredith Robbins in *School Library Journal*. *Jumped* was a finalist for the 2009 National Book Award.

Winning the Coretta Scott King Award

Williams-Garcia created her most recent novel, *One Crazy Summer* (2010), as a work of historical fiction aimed at middle-school readers. It follows three sisters—11-year-old Delphine and her younger siblings Vonetta and Fern—as they travel to Oakland, California, to visit their estranged mother. The story takes place in 1968, an era of radical social change in America, and depicts the Black Panther movement. The Black Panthers group was a militant political party that played a significant role in the civil rights movement, a movement to ban racial discrimination and segregation in the United States. Founded in Oakland in 1966, the Black Panthers sought to protect the African-American community from racism and police brutality, and they were willing to use violence to establish social, political, and economic equality for minorities. The Black Panthers' calls for a revolutionary war against the U.S. government came to the attention of local police and the FBI. These law enforcement officials considered them a threat to the internal security of the nation. But in addition to their violent activities, the Black Panthers created a number of community programs, including free breakfasts for low-income families, clothing drives, and health screenings to test for sickle cell anemia, an inherited blood disorder affecting people of African descent. They also hosted recreational activities for children such as arts and crafts, physical fitness, and literacy.

One Crazy Summer depicts the Black Panther movement from a child's point of view. "I grew up in the 1960s and wanted to share a part of that time with my readers. If we think of the Black Panthers at all, we rarely remember their work with and for children," the author explained. Through Delphine's eyes, the reader experiences the pivotal changes of that period in history as she and her sisters attend a summer camp sponsored by the Black Panthers.

One Crazy Summer earned Williams-Garcia admiration from critics, who praised her ability to interweave themes of family and identity with broader social issues. "Regimented, responsible, strong-willed Delphine narrates in an unforgettable voice, but each of the sisters emerges as a distinct, memorable character, whose hard-won, tenuous connections with their mother

One Crazy Summer *won a host of awards, including the Coretta Scott King Author Award and the Scott O'Dell Award for Historical Fiction.*

build to an aching, triumphant conclusion," wrote Gillian Engberg in *Booklist*. "Set during a pivotal moment in African-American history, this vibrant novel shows the subtle ways that political movements affect personal lives; but just as memorable is the finely drawn, universal story of children reclaiming a reluctant parent's love." Reviewer Teri Markson offered similar praise in *School Library Journal.* "Emotionally challenging and beautifully written, this book immerses readers in a time and place and raises difficult questions of cultural and ethnic identity and personal responsibility. With memorable characters (all three girls have engaging, strong voices) and a powerful story, this is a book well worth reading and rereading."

One Crazy Summer also earned Williams-Garcia a host of awards. She won the 2011 Coretta Scott King Author Award and the Scott O'Dell Award for Historical Fiction. In addition, the novel was selected as a finalist for the National Book Award and was named a Newbery Honor Book. "[*One Crazy Summer*] was selected because it is thought-provoking and features complex, well developed characters," said Jonda C. McNair, chair of the Coretta Scott King Awards jury.

Williams-Garcia has frequently confronted serious issues in her books. But she has maintained that her main focus is on developing characters. "Although my stories are contemporary and realistic, I don't write specifically about issues. I write about my characters' lives," she said. As critic Carla Sarratt stated in an interview for the website the *Brown Bookshelf*, "Rita connects with her characters and shows us that connection so that we feel as if we really know [them].... She studies people and imagines what if and out of those what if moments, a story is born." While most of her characters and storylines are the result of daydreams, she injects little pieces of herself into each of her characters. For example, she was an avid dancer like Joyce in *Blue Tights,* and she sold candy door-to-door like Denzel in *Fast Talk on a Slow Track.* "The characters have to become part of Rita; they need to talk to her before she can write," affirmed Brosnan, her longtime friend and editor. Despite writing about controversial or sensitive topics like sexual assault and bullying, she considers herself an optimist. "I'm always very hopeful about the generation that's coming up and the avenues that are opening up and how people are discovering that they can make an impact. I'm a very happy, hopeful person."

Advice to Young Writers

Williams-Garcia teaches in the Writing for Children and Young Adults Master of Fine Arts (MFA) program at the Vermont College of Fine Arts. In addition, she holds an annual short story contest for young authors between the ages of 12 and 19 to help develop new talent. She encourages

> ❝
>
> *Williams-Garcia encourages aspiring writers to read as much as possible, to study the techniques that authors use for effective storytelling, and to spend at least 15 minutes a day writing. "Write for your own joy to get into the habit of flexing those muscles," she urged. "Writing a little bit each day will grow into a sustained ability. Just write!"*
>
> ❞

aspiring writers to read as much as possible, to study the techniques that authors use for effective storytelling, and to spend at least 15 minutes a day writing. "Write for your own joy to get into the habit of flexing those muscles," she urged. "Writing a little bit each day will grow into a sustained ability. Just write!" In addition, she has emphasized the importance of paying attention to the surrounding environment using all five senses. "As you engage your senses to the world around you, your word choices and images will become all the more lively and multi-dimensional," she maintained. Finally, she has stressed the importance of understanding grammar to develop good habits and clear, concise sentence structure. She envisions herself focusing on community outreach in the future. In fact, she predicted that "20 years from now, I'll probably direct my resources and energy toward creating a space for other people to write. Most likely, young people."

MARRIAGE AND FAMILY

In the early 1980s Rita married Peter Garcia, with whom she had two daughters, Michelle and Stephanie. Peter served in the Persian Gulf War of 1990-91 when the children were young. The couple later divorced, but Peter remains a close and supportive friend. "Back while I was trying to do everything (work, write, school), my ex-husband kicked in as 'Super Dad,'" she stated. "The marriage didn't hold, but the co-parenting is forever." She lives in Jamaica, Queens, New York.

FAVORITE BOOKS

Williams-Garcia's list of favorite young adult books includes *Skellig,* by David Almond; *A Wrinkle in Time,* by Madeleine L'Engle; *Island of the Blue Dolphins,* by Scott O'Dell; and *The Hobbit,* by J.R.R. Tolkien. As a child, she read the books of Beverly Cleary and particularly enjoyed Louise Fitzhugh's novel *Harriet the Spy.* She has cited Jamaica Kincaid, Gayle Jones, and Toni Cade Bambara as her favorite authors.

Williams-Garcia with two high school students at a book signing.

HOBBIES AND OTHER INTERESTS

Williams-Garcia likes to visit schools to talk to students about her career. Like her character Gayle in *Like Sisters on the Homefront,* she hates to fly, and she refuses to travel by air during the winter months. In her spare time, she enjoys sewing, knitting, playing chess or Tetris, jogging, and boxing at the gym. She loves art, especially the works of Pablo Picasso, Vincent Van Gogh, and 20th-century collage artist Romare Bearden. While she is developing the characters for her books, she often listens to music as inspiration. She enjoys many musical genres, including soul, be-bop, gospel, Afro-Brazilian, reggae, and ska. Moreover, she admires such vocalists as Aretha Franklin, Nancy Wilson, Alicia Keyes, Johnny Hartman, and Frank Sinatra. "I love vocalists because I can't carry a note pinned to my sweater," she joked.

SELECTED WRITINGS

Blue Tights, 1987
Fast Talk on a Slow Track, 1991
Like Sisters on the Homefront, 1995
Catching the Wild Waiyuuzee, 2000

Every Time a Rainbow Dies, 2001
No Laughter Here, 2004
Jumped, 2009
One Crazy Summer, 2010

HONORS AND AWARDS

Books Recommended for Reluctant Readers (American Library Association): 1988, for *Blue Tights*; 1992, for *Fast Talk on a Slow Train*; 1996, for *Like Sisters on the Homefront*

Books for the Teen Age (New York Public Library): 1989, for *Blue Tights*; 2002, for *Every Time a Rainbow Dies*

Best Books for Young Adults (American Library Association): 1991, for *Fast Talk on a Slow Track*; 1995, for *Like Sisters on the Homefront*; 2002, for *Every Time a Rainbow Dies*; 2005, for *No Laughter Here*; 2010, for *Jumped*

Best Books for Young Adults (*School Library Journal*): 1995, for *Like Sisters on the Homefront*

Best Books for Young Adults (*Publishers Weekly*): 1995, for *Like Sisters on the Homefront*

Fanfare Award (*Horn Book*): 1995, for *Like Sisters on the Homefront*

NCSS-CBC Notable Books in the Field of Social Studies (National Council for the Social Studies-Children's Book Council): 1996, for *Like Sisters on the Homefront*

PEN/Norma Klein Award for a New Children's Fiction Writer (PEN American Center): 1997, for three books, *Blue Tights, Fast Talk on a Slow Track,* and *Like Sisters on the Homefront*

Best Children's Books for the Year (Bank Street College): 2001, for *Catching the Wild Waiyuuzee*

Top 10 Black History Titles for Youth (*Booklist*): 2004, for *No Laughter Here*

Youth Editors' Choice Award (*Booklist*): 2009, for *Jumped*

Coretta Scott King Author Award (American Library Association): 2011, for *One Crazy Summer*

Scott O'Dell Award for Historical Fiction (American Library Association): 2011, for *One Crazy Summer*

FURTHER READING

Periodicals

Booklist, Feb. 15, 1996, p.1002
Horn Book Magazine, Sep./Oct. 2009, p.479; Mar./Apr. 2011, p.151; July/Aug. 2011, pp.86 and 94.
School Library Journal, May 2010, p.22

Online Articles

www.thebrownbookshelf.com
  (Brown Bookshelf, "Rita Williams-Garcia," Feb. 4, 2008, 28 Days Later archive, 2008)
cynthialeitichsmith.blogspot.com/2009/03
  (Cynsations, Cynthia Leitich Smith, "Author Interview: Rita Williams-Garcia on *Jumped*," Mar. 27, 2009, scroll to correct date)
www.hofstra.edu
  (Hofstra College of Liberal Arts & Sciences: In Focus, "Rita Williams-Garcia '80: Liberal Arts Major," undated, In Focus—University Relations archive)
archive.hbook.com/magazine/articles/2011/jul11_brosnan.asp
  (Horn Book, "Rita Williams-Garcia," July-Aug. 2011)
www.loc.gov
  (Library of Congress 2011 National Book Festival, "Rita Williams-Garcia," 2011, National Book Festival archive, Kids and Teachers site, Meet the Authors category)
www.myshelf.com
  (MyShelf.com, "Rita Williams-Garcia," Feb. 2003, Have You Heard archive, 2003)
www.nationalbook.org
  (National Book Foundation, "Rita Williams-Garcia: *One Crazy Summer*," 2010, National Book Awards 2010 archive, Young People's Literature category)
comminfo.rutgers.edu/professional-development/childlit/AuthorSite/index.html
  (Rutgers University, Kay E. Vandergrift's Learning about the Author and Illustrator Pages, "Learning about Rita William-Garcia: Biography," Sep. 1996)

ADDRESS

Rita Williams-Garcia
Author Mail, 18th Floor
HarperCollins Children's Books
10 East 53rd Street
New York, NY 10022

WEB SITES

www.ritawg.com
www.harpercollins.com/authors/19042/Rita_WilliamsGarcia

Photo and Illustration Credits

Front Cover/Photos: Adele: Vince Bucci/Picture Group via AP Images; Dale Earnhardt Jr.: Jared C. Tilton/Getty Images for NASCAR; Steve Jobs: David Paul Morris/Getty Images; Hilda Solis: U.S. Department of Labor.

Adele/Photos: PR Newswire/Newscom (p. 9); Carmen Valino/PA Photos/Landov (p. 11); Dana Edelson/NBC/NBCU Photo Bank via AP Images (p. 14); XL Recordings/Columbia Records (p. 16); MTV/PictureGroup (p. 18).

Chris Daughtry/Photos: Brendan McDermid/Reuters/Landov (p. 21); Market Wire Photos/Newscom (p. 24); Ray Mickshaw/WireImage (p. 26); Album cover: LEAVE THIS TOWN © 2009 RCA Records/Sony Music Group (p. 29); RCA Records/Sony Music Group (p. 30).

Dale Earnhardt Jr./Photos: John Harrelson/Getty Images for NASCAR (p. 35); Racing Photo Archives/Getty Images (p. 37); Jeff Siner/MCT/Landov (p. 40); Jonathan Ferrey/ALLSPORT/Getty Images (p. 42); Mark Wallheiser/RTR/Newscom (p. 45); Jerry Markland/Getty Images for NASCAR (p. 46); Todd Warshaw/Getty Images (p. 49); Geoff Burke/Getty Images for NASCAR (p. 52).

Heidi Hammel/Photos: NASA/Bill Ingalls (p. 55); Roger L. Wollenberg/UPI/Newscom (p. 58); NASA/JPL (p. 61, top and bottom); NASA/HST (p. 63); H.A. Weaver, T.E. Smith/Space Telescope Science Institute/NASA (p. 65, top); Hubble Space Telescope Comet Team/NASA (p. 65, bottom); NASA/MSFC/David Higginbotham (p. 68, top); NASA (p. 68, bottom).

Steve Jobs/Photos: David Paul Morris/Getty Images (p. 71); Kimberly White/Reuters/Landov (p. 75); SSPL/Getty Images (p. 77, top); Terry Schmitt/UPI/Landov (p. 77, bottom); Movie still: TOY STORY © Disney. All Rights Reserved. (p. 80); AP Photo/Ben Margot (p. 82); © Apple Inc. All rights reserved. (p. 85); Cartoon by Steve Sack. Reprinted with permission, Minneapolis Star Tribune (p. 87); © 2011 Apple Inc. All rights reserved. (p. 89).

Jennifer Lawrence/Photos: Michael Buckner/Getty Images for Jameson (p. 93); Very-Funny Productions/Album/Newscom (p. 95); Movie still: WINTER'S BONE © 2010 Roadside Attractions/DVD distributed by Lionsgate (p. 97); Murray Close/TM and © 2011 Twentieth Century Fox Film Corporation. All rights reserved. (p. 99); Movie still: THE HUNGER GAMES © 2012 Lionsgate. Photo by Murray Close (p. 101); Movie still: THE HUNGER GAMES © 2012 Lionsgate. Photo by Murray Close (p. 102).

Manny Pacquiao/Photos: Danny Moloshok/Reuters/Landov (p. 107); Calabria Design/ Omnigraphics (p. 109); AP Photo/Laura Rauch (p. 114); AP Photo/Eric Jamison (p. 117); Ian Halperin/UPI/Landov (p. 118); AP Photo (p. 120).

AnnaSophia Robb/Photos: Christopher Polk/KCA2011/Getty Images for Nickelodeon (p. 123); Movie still: BECAUSE OF WINN-DIXIE 20th Century Fox/Suzanne Tenner/Album/Newscom (p. 126, top); DVD: SAMANTHA - AN AMERICAN GIRL HOLIDAY © 2011 Warner Home Video. All rights reserved. (p. 126, middle); Movie still: CHARLIE AND THE CHOCOLATE FACTORY © 2005 Warner Bros. Entertainment Inc. All rights reserved. (p. 126, bottom); Movie still: BRIDGE TO TERABITHIA © Buena Vista Home Entertainment, Inc. and Walden Media, LLC. All rights reserved. (p. 128); DVD cover: SOUL SURFER © 2011 Sony Pictures Home Entertainment (p. 130).

Hilda Solis/Photos: U.S. Department of Labor (p. 133); Aurelia Ventura/La Opinion/ Newscom (p. 135); Dan Groshong/AFP/Getty Images (p. 137); AP Photo/Damian Dovarganes (p. 140); Official White House Photo by Pete Souza (p. 143); Jim West/ U.S. Department of Labor (p. 145).

Rita Williams-Garcia/Photos: Courtesy, Rita Williams-Garcia (p. 149, 152); Book cover: BLUE TIGHTS Copyright © 1987 Rita Williams-Garcia (1996 reprint, Puffin Books/ Penguin Group) Courtesy, Rita's website: http://www.ritawg.com/my-books (p. 154); Book cover: LIKE SISTERS ON THE HOMEFRONT Copyright © Rita Williams-Garcia, 1995. All rights reserved. (Puffin Books/Penguin Group). Cover illustration © Dominick Finelle, 1998. Cover design by Stefanie Rosenfeld. (p. 157, top); Courtesy, Rita Williams-Garcia (p. 157, bottom); Book cover: ONE CRAZY SUMMER Copyright © 2010 Rita Williams-Garcia (Amistad/HarperCollins Publishers) Courtesy, Rita's website: http://www.ritawg.com/my-books (p. 160); Courtesy, Rita Williams-Garcia (p. 163).

Cumulative Names Index

This cumulative index includes the names of all individuals profiled in *Biography Today* since the debut of the series in 1992.

For cumulative general, places of birth, and birthday indexes, please see biographytoday.co

For cumulative general, places of birth, and birthday indexes, please see biographytoday.com.

177

For cumulative general, places of birth, and birthday indexes, please see biographytoday.com

For cumulative general, places of birth, and birthday indexes, please see biographytoday.com

For cumulative general, places of birth, and birthday indexes, please see biographytoday.co